Tales of the Tailless

Manx Cat and Kitten at Play.

by Robert Kelly

An Anthology incorporating historic pos.
from the Robert and Linda Kelly collect.

Contents

Are we Downhearted ?
No! Not in the Isle of Man.

Soon be home now. Had a glorious motor ride yesterday in the Sefton car all round the Island. It was 'heavenly'. See you Monday.
Love J.

(Douglas 24 . IX . 11)

"Tales of the Tailless" is produced with the assistance of the Isle of Man Postal Authority whose interest in Manx cats is depicted in the Manx stamp issues on the inside front and inside back covers of the book.

Introduction

Few other cats provoke so much fascination or curiousity. A cat without a tail? Is it a freak or did someone chop it off? Cameras click, people stare.

To the people of the small self-governing Crown Dependency of the Isle of Man, geographically in the centre of the British Isles, it's just a plain Manxie, a normal everyday sight. But to others who see it, it's one of the wonders of the feline world.

When car race pioneer Tom Thornycroft started one of the first T.T. races in the Isle of Man earlier this century he did so with one of his legs strapped up on the side of the car that bore his name. His co-driver had to change the clutch for him. The cause of all his woes - one humble tailless Manx cat. So eager was Thornycroft to see one, he had climbed over a wall and had fallen.

Such is the fascination of the cat. It has no tail - yet has plenty of tales to tell.

The Manx has travelled far and wide, an unwitting ambassador of its original Island home, been the pet of the rich and famous, royalty (and even a gorilla!) and has earned a reputation as being one of the feline world's best hunters.

Books have been inspired by it:; verse too.

There are thousands of besotted owners, particularly in the U.S.A., and there are hundreds of breeders world-wide, many of them with trading names adopted from locations in the cat's original homeland of the Isle of Man.

The Manx has inspired devotion even among hardened seamen.

One January day in 1959 when the Australian inter-state freighter *Cronulla* left Cairns bound for Melbourne, the 48 crew were shocked to discover they had left the ship's tabby Manx cat, Professor, ashore - and she had four kittens aboard the vessel which had to be reared.

As the second engineer fed the kittens with an eyedropper an urgent radio message was sent to the authorities at Cairns - Please find Professor and fly her to Melbourne. The crew would guarantee the fare.

For two days there was no news; then Professor was found and despatched. Sadly one of the kittens died but the other three survived.

So relieved were the crew they piped the returning Professor aboard!

Internationally the Manx cat is rare. Fine specimens have a price on their heads.

Yet in the Isle of Man they're treated mostly as family pets. They roam the streets and by-ways, some nonchalantly posing for the cameras of tourists.

Inevitably some are stolen. In 1966 six show champions

QUOCUNQUE JECERIS

Get out! You've got a tail!

Old Manx Woman and her Spinning Wheel.

MANX LIFE STUDIES.

Kirk Michael 3 . V . 29

vanished in ten days - two of them, Kelly and Basil, the previous year's and that year's Island champions owned by Enid Crellin of Greeba.

In the early 1990s a distraught owner saw her cat being bundled into a car but she was too late to do anything about it. Still, however, the Manxies roam free.

The risk they run is freedom's price and it seems most owners consider it one worth paying.

Manx cats have been show winners ever since the last century.

Rose Tennent who wrote "Pedigree Cats" in 1955 (published by Lockwood and Son Ltd) reported that during the 19th century some very good specimens appeared at shows at Crystal Palace. A particularly memorable one and consistent class winner was a tortoiseshell Manx which was exhibited on a collar and lead like a dog.

The first Manx to be recorded as a champion was a silver tabby called Bonhaki and owned by the keeper of London Zoo, a Mr Brookes.

One of the most perfect rumpies seen at a British show was a tabby female known as Stona Kate (sometimes more affectionately as "Grandma"). Bred and owned by Miss G.K. Sladen, the cat appeared many times on TV and films.

Croydon 27 . XI . 05

Old Manx Woman
and her Cat.

Douglas 28 . VII . 13

Kys ta Shiu ?

We've arrived in the land that is called " the Manx,"
Where the cats have no tails, and are full of their pranks,
We're in for some fun, and we're " very well thanks,

MANX CAT AND KITTENS AT PLAY.

Kys ta Shiu?

The pussies and the " toms," tho' they havent any tails,
Are keenly alive to the pleasures of the "sails";
Not having any tales (don't forget it now)—you know
It's rather longer odds you don't give away the show.

TOWER OF REFUGE

Kys ta Shiu?

QUOCUNQUE JECERIS STABIT

Ellan Vannin, veg veen.

The Forebears of some of the champion Manx cats of today had adventurous young lives.

Black and white footed Cindy, for example, was found after being thrown into a cement mixer at Ramsey.

The kitten had been living rough in cement bags on a building site. Workers emptying the bags into the mixer one day unwittingly emptied her as well - then rescued her.

Legs caked in cement and suffering from a rupture, Cindy was brought by a road cleaner to the home of Sheila and Brian Waiting, then of Jurby and later of Ballavolley Lodge, Ballaugh. He knew of their interest in Manx cats and their breeding of them so reckoned they would provide her with a good home.

So they did. Sheila, a former head teacher at various northern primary schools (the last being Bride) and her husband Brian, former head of biology at Ramsey Grammar School, nursed Cindy back to health and eventually the new arrival rewarded them with some fine rumpies.

The first litter was born in a hole under an old garden elm: ideal for a cat who valued her independence.

One of her kittens was the light green-eyed and all black Sooty, weak at first, two long hind legs stretched out so far behind him that he had to inch forward on his stomach. For a time the Waitings wondered if he would survive. They could scarce imagine then what a sturdy, strong-willed individual he would become: the top Tom among their breeding cats, sire of many magnificent rumpies.

From his mother he inherited an independent streak too, sometimes wandering off for days, even a week, into the countryside hunting for rabbits and pheasant. Once he was shot in the hind quarters by a farmer but he recovered.

Eventually Sooty became a celebrity, filmed by visiting television crews from Russia and Japan.

Freda Williams of Dreemskerry Manx Cattery in the heart of the New Forest at Furzehill, F o r d i n g b r i d g e , Hampshire acquired her first Manx cats in dramatic incidents whilst resident at Regaby on the Island in the 1950s.

One was a kitten trapped in a pound adjoining an empty cottage. She escaped by digging a burrow in the earthen floor. Freda found her in the garden totally exhausted and nursed her back to health.

Another kitten was discovered when walking her dog one day on the beach. Out to sea she saw a black speck bobbing up and down in the water. It proved to be a Manx cat which someone must have thrown into the sea. Freda retrieved the poor thing, exhausted and vomiting, took him home and nursed him back to health.

Miss Bessie Christian of Lezayre

When Freda left the Island she had seven Manx cats and could boast: "I've never had a scratch or bite from one of them."

Images of Manx cats have cropped up in the strangest places . . .

Like in the remote former gold mining village of Pilgrém's Rest in North East Transvaal, South Africa.

Manx people happening by there in the 1980s were astonished to encounter a man carrying a billboard saying: "Don't Miss the Manx Cat."

Investigations revealed this referred to a small art smithy in the village, now being promoted as a tourist attraction. Swinging from its single storey wooden exterior was a sign with a picture of a Manx cat on it.

Why the name? Why the sign? Sadly much of the explanation has been lost with the passage of time - but there are tantalising hints. Nearby there is a peak called "Manx Hill" and more than a hundred years ago someone registered a gold mine there called "The Manx Cat."

It all suggests that a Manxman passed that way and maybe struck it rich.

Or . . . did he die tragically, his only bequest to the villagers who knew nothing of the Isle of Man, the strange name and emblem?

Certainly in the local cemetery there can be found the grave of a certain John Thomas Kelly. He died in January, 1876 . . . and there, presumably, hangs a tale of a different sort!

According to the Standard Library of Natural History, published in New York in 1909, tailless cats were once known as Cornwall cats. Only later did they become known as Manx.

One source on which the publishers probably relied was Baron Cuvier. In 1827 in his book "Animal Kingdom" he said that tailless cats were "not uncommon" in Cornwall. There had even been a specimen found in the Isle of Wight. Curiously he didn't mention the Isle of Man.

Ten years later Bell's "History of British Quadropeds," said that a considerable number of tailless cats existed both in the Isle of Man and Cornwall.

What it omitted was the link between the two places which would have explained much for cat-lovers elsewhere.

The fact was that many Cornish tin miners worked occasionally in the Isle of Man's lead and silver mines, once among the richest in the British Isles. Not all settled as permanent residents. Those who returned to Cornwall probably took pet cats with them and in so doing transferred the gene for taillessness to their area where in time, not having the restrictions of a small island, it became diluted.

OH!——OH!——OH!——OH!—Flanagan

Just a Line from Douglas.

Types of Manx cat

THERE are four distinct types of Manx cat:

- *Dimple Rumpies;*
- *Rumpy Risers;*
- *Stumpies; and*
- *Longies.*

"*Dimple Rumpies*" are the purest. There is not the slightest hint of a tail as they do not have any coccygeal vertebrae. Where a tail would emerge there is a dimple into which the tip of a finger can be slotted.

In the early '50s Liverpool University researchers said male rumpies were particularly rare. It was suspected that most of them died *in utero.*

"*Rumpy Risers*" have a bump at the end of their spinal columns. Researchers in the U.S.A. have revealed that the cats have some coccygeal vertebrae usually fused in an upright position. Some cats can have a tuft of fur growing like a rosette on a small fold of skin on their rumps and this has been confused sometimes as the beginnings of a tail. At early British cat shows some judges penalised exhibited cats because of it.

"King Clinkie" became a celebrity when judges claimed that this was the beginnings of a stub. Other cat fanciers including cartoonist Louis Wain, examined him and said it was only a tuft. Later "King Clinkie" became a champion.

It is a tufted Manx that has been displayed in the Natural History department of the Manx Museum in Douglas for at least fifty years. The cat isn't a particularly remarkable specimen other than for the unusually pale beige fur with light black marbling. The fact that it was chosen as an example of its variety, however, suggests that the tuft was a common occurrence.

Prior to Isle of Man shows it has been known for exhibitors to cut any tufts off. However, Mrs May Teare (manageress of the first Manx Cattery at Knockaloe Experimental Farm and a show judge thereafter) insisted: "I can tell when the fluff's been cut. It leaves a blunt mark on the fur."

"*Stumpies*" (sometimes called "Stubbies") have the beginnings of a tail; usually the powder-puff type like that of a rabbit. Several coccygeal vertebrae sometimes have a kink in them. Some American breeders have been known to remove the stumps at birth but not all removals have been through a human agency. Dr E. C. Herdman MSc of Liverpool University reported in 1930 at a meeting of the Antiquarian Society in Douglas that she had seen a long-tailed mother of a stumpy "bite off the piece that she apparently considered untidy" when cleaning the kitten.

Mrs Sheila Quaggin of Ballakayt Manx, Woodbourne Road, Douglas got a shock in 1993 when a three month old stumpy shed part of his stump when she lifted him out of a box. He had been born with a twisted stump. Apparently there had been a natural constriction in the final twisted section with the result that as he had grown the end part of the stump had failed to develop. Eventually it just fell off.

Nature in a mood of Sport,
Built our tails a trifle short,
But we're true Mascots, bear in mind,
And bring Good Luck, as you will find.
So keep us Pussies if you can,
With Greetings from the Isle of Man.
A.P.C.

Douglas 12 . VII . 21

"*Longies*," sometimes known as "Taillies" in the Isle of Man, have full length tails but have all the other characteristics of a Manx cat in respect of coat and long hind legs. Many also carry the gene for taillessness so can pass it on to their descendants.

In the past some breeders recommended the killing of Longies at birth to give tailless kittens a better chance of survival in a litter. This happened on occasions in the early days of the Manx Cattery. Others docked the tails to make them more popular to buyers though there was no question of "passing off" the cats as pure Manx. Veterinary certificates provided with the cats confirmed what had happened.

Today British vets won't dock a tail without there being a medical reason for doing so.

Historically it would seem that the original Manx cats were not totally tailless.

The Rev Theophilus Talbot who made a study of them on the Isle of Man last century observed: Though people spoke of taillessness "there are, in all probability, no cats here which are utterly tailless. I have not seen one. In specimens which approach the nearest to the tailless state there is a portion of tail; a rudimentary continuation of the backbone, however small."

His observations are borne out by the experiences last century of cat judge Harrison Weir, president of Britain's National Cat Club. In a list of "Points of Excellence," published in 1889, he observed: "Some true bred have a very short, thin, twisted tail that cannot be straightened." This was allowable in shows, he thought, though "thick stumps, knobs or short thick tails," were not.

Five years later he examined a number of specimens sent to an exhibition at Crystal Palace, London and other cat shows. He found some to have very short, thin and twisted tails; others to have a "mere excrescence" and some with an appendage like a knob.

He dismissed them all as not being real Manx cats. The truth, however, may have been the reverse: that the dimple rumpy is the product of deliberate breeding whilst the natural state is stumpiness.

Hence the original Manx name for a tailless cat; a "stubbin" - that is, one which has a stub.

The Tragedy of the Manx cat

The tragedy of the Manx cat is the very cause of its existence. It's a mutation. That means all sorts of things can go wrong.

On one occasion at the Manx Cattery in Noble's Park one kitten was born with a hare lip, the first time local vets had encountered the problem.

Paralysis in the rear legs or an absence of complete movement in them is another handicap.

Depressingly more common are the twin problems of constipation and leaking bowels.

Occasionally with care and certain diets based on extra roughage to "tone up" the bowel, weakling kittens have been raised to become sturdy adults. But for many there is nothing that can be done and they have had to be put down. The administration of liquid paraffin, a traditional treatment for constipation, only aggravates the condition.

Manx vet Frank Wadsworth of Ballasalla, a breeder of Manx cats since 1978, believes dimple rumpies to be the most susceptible. The shorter the spinal column the greater the likelihood that the necessary nerve linkages between the spinal vertebrae and vital organs such as the bowel and bladder won't develop. When they don't the cats so afflicted can suffer chronic constipation. The mass within the bowel gains volume, begins to ferment and liquify and this then oozes from the cat giving the impression that it is suffering from diarrhoea.

In the case of feral cats the misery can be worsened by soiled fur attracting flies and the hatching of maggots from their eggs.

It is because of problems such as this that the deliberate breeding of Manx cats to perpetuate the variety has been criticised. There have been suggestions in the E.E.C. that pedigree breeding should be banned.

However, it is possible that controlled breeding has helped to make the problems less common. Substantially higher success rates for healthy kittens are being reported.

When he started breeding Manx cats in 1978 Mr Wadsworth decided that the bowel and hind leg problems were attributable to a recessive gene caused by long-practised in-breeding among uncontrolled farm cats. His policy was to "breed-away" from that background by introducing new blood and the birth since then of successive generations of healthy tailless tabbies seems to have confirmed his diagnosis.

Other breeders have reported similar successes.

Many Manx cats may be weak at birth but those who survive kittenhood can be tough. They have earned a reputation of being excellent rabbiters.

Within the Christian family of Milntown, Lezayre there was a legend that centuries ago Manx cats roamed wild on the hills behind the ancient Viking fortress. Indeed, some still do.

Manx historian Mona Douglas, a cat lover all her life, wrote in May 1963: "Mother cats who have lost one or two litters at human hands on a farm sometimes go away to have the next one and bring the kittens up wild. In unfrequented places these cat colonies may sometimes be glimpsed and they are nearly always rumpies."

During the 1950s Mona managed to tame a tabby rumpy she befriended on the brooghs surrounding Bulgham Bay.

"It took about six months and a lot of patience," she recalled later, "but in the end I was able to get it home. It became quite affectionate with me but nobody else could get a hand on it and it still spent most of its time out hunting."

Mona called it Keoje, meaning Wild.

Not all good hunters are wild by nature, however. Ginger, a large rumpy owned in the 1980s by the

These Victorian "Manx tabbies" depicted on a white cotton headscarf produced in the early 1870s look healthy. Sadly, however, not all were.

operators of the now closed J.R.'s Restaurant and Tea Rooms opposite the parish church in Bride Village, was a perfect example of a cat which loved both lives.

At home he basked in the admiration of the thousands of tourists who visited the restaurant and its sunken garden where he would lie lazily on a hot summer's day and enjoy being petted. To all intents and purposes he had all he needed at home, no need to wander. But that's just what he did. At night he wandered the fields rabbiting. That's why he was so magnificent, reckoned his owners.

The tendency for some Manx rumpies to have leaking bowels has led to the belief that their disorder is linked to cow's milk.

In some cases it may well be - but it is not a problem exclusive to Manx cats as Isle of Man vet Stuart Angus explains: "A lot of cats are allergic to milk and dairy products. They are unable to digest them."

The problem, therefore, is not one of breed or variety but of individual characteristics.

Milk is not the cause of the general bowel weakness in Manx cats, just the creator of similar symptoms in certain individuals. Hence the differing opinions on milk over the years.

Manx Government Vet Douglas Kerruish said in the 1970s that he had been told by farmers that cow's milk didn't suit Manx cats. It caused diarrhoea so they should be weaned onto a non-milk diet. However, he reported: "I have always weaned my kittens on cow's milk without any undue trouble."

Jessie Twining of Greeba, foremost Isle of Man breeder in the 1950s, dismissed the perceived milk problem as nonsense. In fact, she recommended creamy milk for kittens. The problem was, she suggested, that some kittens were not watched closely enough. Manx kittens needed "special care" for the first three months and some degree of care even until they were six months old. Some could suffer from constipation and a form of diarrohea as a result of this. Those suffering from this should be given slightly warmed Benger's Food along with two teaspoonfuls of creamy milk. For a chill she recommended a few drops of brandy in a teaspoonful of warm water.

Forty-five years later Sylvia Church of the Manx Cattery near Orpington in Kent warned: Milk should be given only as a special treat. She gave her cats water, she said. "What do cats do in the wild? They go to a river, not a cow."

In 1966 Mrs C. S. Colville, a successful breeder who lived at Bergholt House in Stanford-le-Hope, Essex, thought the issue wasn't simply milk but rather what sort of milk. She gave her kittens goat's milk and they seemed to thrive on it. One of her cats was the champion all-white Brumas who appeared on T.V. and film commercials for cat foods.

Dairy farmer Mary Corkish of Ballawattleworth whose Manx cats have travelled the world since the 1970s has plenty of fresh milk to draw upon. In fact, her adult cats get between four to five pints a day, poured into bowls by her husband straight from the milking parlour. But her kittens get barely a drop.

It's a lesson she learned long ago, she said. When some of her first Manx kittens suffered from leaking bowels her husband told her: Stop giving them milk. She did and they improved. Ever since she has given her kittens lukewarm water with just a dash of milk in it and there have been no more problems.

Sadly not all kittens afflicted with leaking bowels grow out of the problem. Some of the worst-affected are put down. However, the Ellan Vannin Cat Protection Trust has found homes for some. Whilst unsuited for living in houses, says Laurel Collis (one of its trustees), places such as stables can provide an ideal environment.

The Trust believes that diet can help ease constipation problems. Its recommended diet is: No milk, dry foods with added bran to help the bowel function and plenty of fish and white meat.

Judy Corrin, Animal Welfare Officer for the Manx Society for the Prevention of Cruelty to Animals, doesn't believe in milk either; nor beef or offal. A careful study of the most beneficial diets for the Manx cats she has bred has revealed raw fish to be the best food. "It seems to suit their digestive system better," she said.

Mrs Joan Mann, wife of former chairman of Tynwald's Executive Council Dr Edgar Mann, and a member of the Island's Pets Aids League, can confirm it from personal experience.

One day she came across a semi-feral six month old black rumpy lying in a gutter at Laxey suffering from the effects of chronic constipation. He was in a bad state after relying on what scraps he could get from a local cafe. She took him to a vet experienced in Manx cats and he warned: The cat had only a 50-50 chance of survival. Try giving him bran. Some roughage might work.

Mrs Mann gave him that but was having a difficult time until one day the newly named Sooty misbehaved.

Mrs Mann had a nice piece of raw cod ready to cook for her husband as his tea. Sooty pinched it and ate the lot, even the bone.

That gave her the idea: Wasn't that the sort of food a cat would eat in the wild - the skin and bone all the roughage it would need? Thereafter she fed Sooty nothing else but raw fish; sometimes cod, other times joints of coley from the petshop. Sooty crunched through everything and never looked back. He grew into a big butch cat and lived until he was ten when he was knocked down by a car.

Ever since Mrs Mann has fed all her other cats raw fish and they too, have prospered.

The problems with Manx Cats has prompted medical research.

When the Manx Cattery was being established at Knockaloe in the early sixties a researcher arrived from Guy's Hospital in London.

His request was a grim one: three dead Manxies: one a kitten, one about six months old and another, an adult.

Eventually Mrs May Teare who ran the Cattery was able to oblige. A kitten had been born dead at the Cattery, a young cat had been found dead after being run-over by a car in Atholl Street, Peel; then an adult, a ginger tom, was found lying dead in a road after being the victim of a road accident.

The ultimate fate of the cats was dissection. Researchers had begun to suspect that taillessness in Manx cats could be linked to spina bifida in humans. An orthopaedic surgeon had noticed similarities in the human condition of spina bifida and certain Manx cats, notably the 'dimple rumpy' type.

Later the spines of other Manx cats which had had to be euthanased because of extreme difficulties in co-ordination of their hind legs were removed and sent for examination.

Mr Kerruish reported: "Some are unable to trot or even walk but can travel quite rapidly in a straight line. Corners and sudden turns are sometimes difficult for them and they may stagger or fall when attempting them, particularly if the weak leg is on the outside of the corner."

In rare cases, said Mr Kerruish, both hind legs were affected and a kitten then bore its weight on the forelegs. With its rear legs it could only hop and then it could fall over.

In the USA and Canada in the 1970s breeders donated healthy Manx cats for test breeding. 'Abnormal' cats were given for euthanasia and it was claimed that subsequent dissection identified some cases of spina bifida occulta.

Douglas Kerruish reported locally, however, that British investigations revealed that Manx cat abnormalities were not "exactly" the same as those found in children, only similar.

All Pals at DOUGLAS I.O.M.

The cat that became a symbol

THREE of the most easily recognised symbols of the Isle of Man were captured in this 1911 cartoon in the Liverpool Courier: the Three Legs of Man on the padlock, the bunch of keys representing the House of Keys and the Manx cat.

Of the three, probably the cat is the most known internationally. Hence its use to promote the Island.

When Esther Rantzen of B.B.C. TV's popular Sunday night programme "That's Life!" posed the question in 1979: How many Kellys are there in the Isle of Man a film crew came to investigate. Anyone with the name of Kelly was invited to present themselves on Douglas promenade at a certain time and the film crew would record them walking past the camera saying: "Hello. I'm Kelly!"

Inevitably when members of the Kelly clan responded they found themselves joined by two kitten rumpies - both called Kelly - brought from the Douglas Corporation's Cattery at Noble's Park at the instigation of Gardens Superintendant Peter Dunn. The show couldn't go on without them, he thought.

The Manx cat was too much of a symbol of the Isle of Man; a reminder to people that this was a place of fascinating differences. Wasn't that one of the reasons why one of the frequent features of the sunken gardens on the seafront was a bed of bright leafed flowers in the shape of a rumpy?

Thus was expressed in a simple act the reality that the rumpy has become more than just a cat: more a symbol of

the Isle of Man, every bit as important as the Three Legs in its coat of arms.

Throughout the world there are thousands who know of the Island who wouldn't but for their cats.

In February 1951 when Douglas furniture removals firm, A. E. Corkill, moved Captain A. H. Hill (the new Cunard Line's Marine Superintendent) from Douglas to New York the backs of the two removal vehicles depicted large grinning Manx cats with the message: "The Isle of Man for Happy Holidays." In this was demonstrated the Island's close association with tailless cats.

Hence the use of the cat as a marketing tool by various businesses earlier this century. A subsidiary company owned by Clucas' Laundry at Tromode produced and marketed Manx Cat brushes, made during the winter to keep their seasonal laundry staff employed. In the 1920s and '30s another company manufactured firelighters and marketed them as "Fargher's Manx Cat Firelytes." Advertisements promised that these would "get the fire going quickly."

Hence too the incorporation of an all-black rumpy along with the outline of the Isle of Man in the badge of the Island's Federation of Young Farmers' Clubs. As the origins of many Manx

cats are traceable to farms it seemed appropriate to use a rumpy as part of the Federation's symbol.

In the 1970s the then chairman of the Tourist Board, Clifford Irving, insisted on having a Manx cat brought to all meetings with visiting press and travel agents; even at evening functions. More than anything else, he knew, the cat's taillessness could intrigue and demonstrate the Island's differences.

For a time give-away stickers to promote the Isle of Man featured a rumpy black cat. Wear them "for luck," recipients were told and some did. Still being marketed along with Manx cat ear rings, pendants, weather vanes are enamel badges combining a black rumpy with the other traditional symbol of the Island, the Three Legs.

In August 1952 17-year-old brown haired wages clerk Bette Upton from Barnham wore one when crowned queen of Eastergate Carnival. "It's my lucky mascot," she said.

She had worn it when selected as queen from 50 others.

A large poster produced in collaboration between the Island's

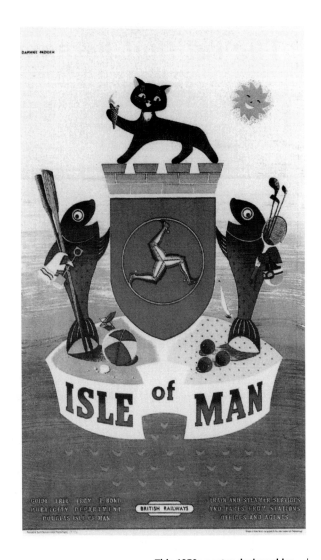

This 1950s poster designed by Daphne Padden relies heavily on symbols to promote the Isle of Man as a holiday resort. It was published jointly by the Publishing Department of British Railways and the I.O.M. Steam Packet Company, and was displayed in railway stations throughout Britain.

We are Cats of the Manx
With our very best thanks
That the tricks of the naughty boys fail

To swing us around,
For no tail can be found,
So their tricks by the tail can't prevail.

Ellan Vannin

Kys ta Shiu?

Tourist Board and the Steam Packet Company, to promote the Isle of Man as a holiday resort featured a large Manx tabby standing on an outline of the Island and waving a greeting across the sea.

Promotional films have featured the cats too. One 20 minute colour travelogue produced in VistaVision in 1958 by Drummer Films in a Country Pride series and narrated by actor Robert Beatty was even given the title "The Isle and the Pussy Cat." A copy is still in the Tourist Department's film library.

Thus we have one of the principal explanations why the tailless mutation has become more than just a passing phenomenon.

P. M. C. Kermode, president of the Isle of Man Natural History and Antiquarian Society in the 1930s, had no doubt about it. This "ugly deformity," he said, had been preserved by human agency; partly from commercial motives but also because of some idea that the deformity would give the Isle of Man a fine advertisement. Personally it was a view with which he had no sympathy.

Of course, sometimes the association doesn't work. People have recognised the name Manx but have never heard of the Isle of Man.

In 1933 the Windsor Ontario Manx Society received a letter from a local cat owner shortly before the North American Manx Association Convention in Detroit.

The letter's request: "I own a Manx cat but I have no pedigree as it was given me. Please send me particulars and kindly keep me on your mailing list."

Clearly the sender had no idea that the Manx Society had nothing to do with cats but rather expatriates of the Isle of Man!

The Manx cat's taillessness even helped the Isle of Man's Second World War war effort - indirectly.

To help promote fund-raising on the Island to pay for the building of Spitfire fighter planes local cartoonist "Dusty" Miller produced this poster of one of the aircraft.

Significantly only the front half is visible for the slogan in the Island of tailless cats was:

"May the enemy never see its tail!"

How did the Manx cat lose its Tail?

A door closes painfully on a cat's tail. Is that how a rumpy is made?

The early comic postcard proved to be the forerunner of many issued by publishers such as Valentine and Salmond which offered alternative possibilities.

A tail was shot off by a blunderbus after a cat had yowled too long one night and kept someone awake.

It was severed by a racing motorcycle in the T.T. races.

It was cut off too by the wheels of a Douglas horse tram - or chopped off by an inattentive butcher.

A Victorian "magic lantern" slide showed a three-legged publican slicing off tails at the bar. At the pub's entrance was a sign: "Manx Cats For Sale".

Towards the end of the Second World War, in 1944, Punch magazine carried a cartoon showing people buying their rations.

A mother and daughter queuing to get theirs saw a rumpy cat washing itself. On the girl pointing to it the mother said: "It's Manx, dear. They haven't any tails."

Puzzled, the girl replied: "Will they in peace time, mummy?"

The inference was that in the child's mind Manx cats went without tails because of the shortages which made so many people do without so much.

It was just one more angle to the age-old puzzle: How did Manx cats lose their tails?

Was it because:
• They were chopped off accidentally and the shock made them breed that way?
• They were lopped off deliberately to make them "different" and so more valuable to sell?
• Mother cats bit them off kittens at birth because ancient warriors killed cats to decorate themselves with furry tales? *or . . .*
• Was it the result of an amorous encounter between a 'mum' puss and a buck rabbit?

All have been suggested, many seriously, especially when the theory of genetics wasn't understood.

The question was raised even in London's House of Commons. But Financial Secretary to the Treasury, Walter Elliot, didn't have the answer.

At a sitting in March 1932 the House was considering some legislation dealing with Customs and Excise in the Isle of Man whereupon Welshman Rhys Davies argued the case for the Celtic Manx to be able to decide Customs rates themselves. They should have the right of free trade, he argued, ignoring the fact that the Island had a voluntary Customs Union agreement with the U.K.

Explaining the Island's differences he said the cats in the Isle of Man were noted for not having tails.

Wearily the Secretary replied: The

How Manx Cats are made

A fearful Cat-astrophe!

legislation didn't extend Custom duties to cat tails whereupon Mr Davies asked mischieviously: Why, then, did the cats have no tails?

The Secretary didn't reply.

Clearly he hadn't studied Manx legends otherwise he would have had an answer.

The most popular hearkens back to the building of Noah's Ark. When the flood came and the animals were led two-by-two aboard the vessel two cats had a typical Manx attitude - "Traa-dy-Liooar," they said (Time enough) then tried to dash aboard at the last moment. Unfortunately the door slammed shut on their tails, chopped them off and ever since their descendants have been tailless.

Alternative theories have included one that the ancient Celts believed that if someone trod on a cat's tail it would become a viper. Consequently when a tailless cat was born it was encouraged to mate and produce more like it.

Another story suggests that Irish warriors who were always raiding the Island wore fur on their shields and helmets. Manx warriors responded by cutting off cat tails to decorate their shields and eventually the cats stopped being born with them.

Even as late as the 1890s there were many who believed such a possibility. When the Rev Theophilus Talbot researched the background to Manx cats he encountered a number of people who believed that the act of cutting off a tail encouraged cats eventually to be born without them. He cited examples of cats which had lost their tails in accidents and which had subsequently given birth to stumpies or rumpies. One

female cat had her tail amputated after a cartwheel ran over it. Subsequently she had two litters in which there were stumpies. A Manx poulterer named Watson told him a story of a local joiner who had his dinner stolen by a cat. When next he saw her he took his revenge with a hatchet by lopping off her tail. Subsequently she gave birth to tailless kittens. The occurrence of the phenomen after the accident, it was suggested, seemed to indicate that "in the perpetuation of an accidentally deformed condition we have the example of the origination of a new variety."

Some people even today believe that Manxies have their tails chopped off.

Ballaugh breeders Sheila and Brian Waiting had a laugh one T.T. race week when a race fan hurried to them and said: "Quick, mister. There's a cat up a tree and the dogs have had its tail already!"

Then there's the story of a mother who brought her young son into the Manx Cattery at Noble's Park shortly after it opened. The boy expected to see the tail of the top tom, Tiger, hung up on a wall!

The notion is not so fanciful as it first seems.

Earlier this century there was an area in France known as Eifell where most cats were tailless. Peasants chopped them off because they believed there was a worm in the tail which reduced a cat's mousing abilities.

There was a suspicion on the Isle of Man too in the 1880s that not all cats sold to visitors as being Manx were truly so. Ten shillings for an adult and five shillings for a kitten was a lot in those days - certainly enough to tempt the unscrupulous to manufacture the required cats.

Observed the Rev Theophilus

Provisionally Protected, No. 20102

M. N. CO. S.

GREAT MISSIONARY MEETING

MONDAY NEXT AT 7.30 p.m.

PRINCE CHIOKIOKIZZA

THE CANNIBAL CHIEF

WILL TELL

THE TALE OF HIS LIFE

ILLUSTRATED BY LANTERN VIEWS.

ADMISSION 1/-

I WONDER IF THEY WOULD LIKE TO SEE MINE.

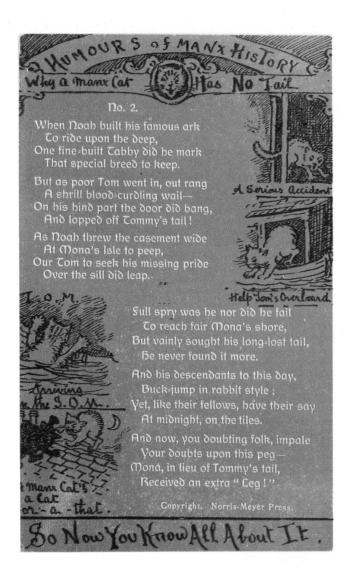

Norris Meyer Press of Douglas issued this postcard version of how the Manx cat lost its tail about 1906 – 1908.

Talbot: "Nature does not provide tailless cats quite so fast and surely as some persons deem desirable and so art is called to the assistance of nature."

American author and cat fancier Milan Greer who wrote "The Fabulous Feline" in 1960-61 after studying the moods and behaviour of 15,000 cats had an awkward moment once because someone believed he had de-tailed some cats. He wrote afterwards: "I used to stock Manxes occasionally but I stopped when some neighborhood busy-body reported me to the American Society for the Protection of Cruelty to Animals for cutting the tails off helpless cats."

This proved to be the last straw for him, he said. Manx cats had given him the "heebie jeebies" already because of their "martyr complex."

"Manx cats, I swear, are the most doleful, dependant animals on four legs," he declared. "They stare at you with those great, soulful, sorrowing eyes until you start wondering whether you did cut off their tails."

Milan Greer may have been innocent of the charge but others were not.

As the Rev Talbot suspected, some hotel porters and others at Douglas at the turn of the century did dock the tails of normal cats so they could be sold to gullible tourists as holiday souvenirs. The practice became so bad that there were suggestions that the Manx Parliament, Tynwald, should amend the Adulteration Act to provide a legal definition of a Manx cat and so make it illegal to sell "doctored" ones.

This didn't happen but local breeders, anxious to protect their reputations, did introduce a system for a time whereby veterinary certificates were provided with their kittens to the effect that there had been no docking of tails.

Occasionally docking is a medical necessity; after an accident, for example, where tails are broken.

This has resulted in non-Manx cats which have suffered in this way sometimes being mistaken as Manx.

Chris Tovell, assistant financial controller of the Manx Treasury, once had a black cat with a white bib known as Humphrey. After being injured in a road accident in Douglas, Humphrey had his tail docked.

Afterwards, said Chris, he spotted a number of tourists "creeping up the drive to our house to take pictures of Humphrey. They didn't realise he wasn't a Manx cat."

Probably the most enduring explanation of the Manx cat's origins, so far as the Isle of Man is concerned, is that the cat was an immigrant brought to the Island by the accident of shipwreck, its tail lost already somewhere else.

Curiously it is a myth repeated in

A Danish – born Manx cat – Quintessenza Clou – pictured at eight months old in 1987

"*Noah sailing on the sea stuck hard and fast on Ararat.*
His dog then made a grab and took The tail from off a pretty cat.
Puss through the window then did fly And swam as only brave cats can;
Nor never stopped 'till, high and dry,
She landed on the Calf of Man.
Then tailless puss earned Mona's thanks
And for ever after was called Manx."

— **Verse from booklet about the Manx cat published in 1882 by Joseph Johnson of Douglas.**

Denmark to explain the presence there of tailless cats - in what used to be a quaint village with similarities to Dalby. Reerso lies between Funen and Zealand, about 100 kms from Copenhagen, connected to the mainland by a narrow strip of land. The cats are not Reersorians though. They're Manx!

According to local cat fanciers in the 1950s the cat colony began when a Manx vessel, name unknown, was wrecked on the island's coast in the mid-19th century.

The truth, however, is more likely to be that the founders of the cat colony probably didn't get to Reerso until the mid-1930s.

Alderman James Skillicorn (Mayor of Douglas between 1933-35) once claimed responsibility.

Whilst he was Mayor, he said, Douglas Corporation received a letter from The Ancient College, Skodsburg to the effect that there were no known Manx cats in Denmark, not even in a zoo. The writer wondered if this deficiency could be remedied and so it was. Hotel porter, George Cave,

When Noah built his famous ark
    To ride upon the deep,
On one fine cat he set his mark,
    That special breed to keep;

"For you see," said he, to his family,
    Before they all set sail,
"No bird, or beast did I ever see
    Adorned with such a tail."

Now the cat had really a lovely tail,
    And with wide and graceful sweep,
He would swing it round like a threshing-fail
    When the flies disturbed his sleep.

But misfortune came, I'm loth to say,
    A sad tale must be told,
And if you will due attention pay,
    I'll now that tale unfold.

                * * * *

Now the birds and beasts of every kind
    Came thronging to the Ark,
In order that none should be left behind
    They must at once embark;
And our gallant Tom of course had a mate
    (Of that you may be sure,)
And said she, "Now Tommy, don't let's be late,"
    But Tommy said, "Traa-dy-Liooar,"*

But Tom was cute, you may all go bail,
    As any modern youth,
Quite keen on guarding himself and his tail
    From the beak and claw and the tooth,
For his kindred folks were all on the list
    In that first gigantic zoo;
The order was that none should be missed,
    For of each there were only two.

And thus it chanced that Tom was the last
    Of all that mighty throng,
For had he gone in with the first that passed
    I'd never writ this song;
As oft it is charged to cruel fate
    By the tardy folks who fail,
Our Tom was the merest trifle late
And the door chopped off this tail!

Oh sad disaster that befel
Poor Tom in that awful bump,
    The door had done its work well,
For it left him never a stump;
    And ye good folks all, due warning take,
In a race never risk delay,
    For he who elects to sail in the wake
Must surely the penalty pay.

Now the Ark went cruising far and wide
    With all its rank and file,
Until one fine morning Noah spied
    A lovely little Isle;
"It was surely here that the dove had stopped,"
    He observed to his little crew;
It was Mona's Isle — and the window he dropped
    To obtain a clearer view.

Now Tom, just roused from a mournful trance,
    Had also gained a peep,
And to seek for his tail there was his chance,
    Then he boldly out did leap,
And deeply sank in the surging main
    From the view of all that host;
But they never saw him rise again,
    So they gave him up for lost.

But Tom was spry, nor did he fail
    To reach fair Mona's shore,
But vainly sought for his missing tail,
    He never beheld it more;
Then he vowed that he nevermore would roam,
    Here was his domicile,
Thenceforward would he make his home
    This fair and lovely Isle.

Now Tom's mishaps his form deranged,
    His hindpart took a hump,
The loss of his appendage changed
    His old-time trot for jump;
And his descendants to this day,
    Progress in rabbit style,
Yet like all cats, they have their say
    At Midnight — on the tile!

Now this is how it came about
    That the Manx cat has no tail,
Yet he seems to get on quite well without,
    For he's always hearty and hale;
And ye doubting folks who wont believe,
    Dispel your doubts, I beg,
For the lost tail Mona will never grieve
    While she boasts of an extra "leg"!

(W. H. Gill, who composed the Manx National Anthem
and the Manx Fisherman's Evening Hymn, composed
this little-known poem about the Manx cat in 1911).

otherwise known as the Manx Cat King because he bred so many in Douglas, was asked to send some cats on behalf of the Corporation and he despatched two females and two males.

Alderman Skillicorn presumed that the Reerso cats were descendants of that gift. By the autumn of 1992, however, the colony's Manxness was in such danger of being lost that Reerso appealed to the Isle of Man for new stock to "build up the blood."

What makes the Reerso experience so fascinating is the explanation as to how Manx cats got there. It's a mirror image of the Isle of Man's own tradition.

This claims that the cats came with the Spanish Armada in 1588. A galleon was wrecked on the Manx coast at a spot known ever since as Spanish Head. Unfortunately there is no historic evidence of such a wreck so most historians have dismissed it as pure invention.

The Rev Theophilus Talbot of Douglas who investigated the story last century concluded in 1883: "I have good reason for saying that little or no confidence can be placed in what persons generally may say on the point . . . " He reckoned that the Spanish Armada story originated only about 35 years earlier and was an invention. Early maps named the supposed site of the wreck as Spalorek, he said. It was only after the tradition of the wreck was popularised that the site became known as Spanish Head.

The possibility that the story is partially accurate remains, however. What seems to have occurred in Victorian times is the romanticising of a wreck to link it to the Armada, thereby obscuring the actual incident.

In 1820, as a young student, the Rev W. B. Clarke of Parkstone, Dorset encountered a totally different account of the wreck which has been overlooked ever since because of the more appealing tale of the Armada. Writing to the magazine of Natural History in 1834 under the heading "A Few Words on Cats," he recalled that whilst on the Island with College friends in the long vacation of 1820 they had "much amusement" with the curious tailless cats.

"I saw several in the huts of the peasantry," he said, "amongst the mountains between Ramsey and Peel Town but as the honest people did not speak English and we spoke no Manx I learned nothing of their history there. But mentioning the subject to a person at Balla Salla near Castle Rushen and not very far from the Calf I was informed that a vessel from Prussia or some part of the Baltic was wrecked many years ago on the rocky shore between Castle Rushen and the Calf and that on her driving close in to the land two or three cats without tails made their escape from the bowsprit and were taken by the wreckers and that these were the first of the kind ever seen in the Island. I don't say that this is the truth but I was told so."

If not from a wreck, from where did the Manx cat come and when?

Modern opinion is that a mutation occurred in the Isle of Man between two and three hundred years ago and the gene gradually spread through the cat population, creating a tendency for taillessness.

It can't have happened too long ago

SPANISH HEAD AND THE
CALF OF MAN.—I.O.M.

for various reasons. For example, had the rumpies developed in historic times one would expect the traditional Manx Gaelic language to have a name for them but it doesn't; only an anglicised "Stubbin."

One would expect Manx legends to tell about Manx cats too - but they don't. There are cat stories, of course; that they have their king who is an ordinary house cat during the day but assumes regal powers at night. People seen ill-treating cats used to be warned: Beware. That could be 'the king of the cats.'

Traditional rhymes don't refer to taillessness either. One sung at Hallowe'en about Jinny the Witch includes the verse:

"Tra-la-laa, I met a wild cat,
Hop-tu-naa, the cat began to grin,
Tra-la-laa, then I began to run..."

If tailless cats had been around when that had been composed one would have expected there to have been special reference to it.

Similarly, one would have expected a "respectful" name for such a strange animal. Manx people didn't believe in calling many creatures by their correct names. It was considered disrespectful, even unlucky, because the super-stitious never could decide whether the animal was truly what it appeared to be or a witch who, according to the Island's Druid beliefs, had the powers to transform herself into the form of other creatures.

Thus a rat, even to this day, is often referred to as a "Long Tail."

If rumpies had been around when such beliefs took root wouldn't there be a tradition for them to be known as "No Tails" or something similar? Instead, the only traditional alternative name is

screebeyder meaning "scratcher".

All this indicates that Manx cats made their appearance within the last few centuries when the Isle of Man was being anglicised but sufficiently long ago for them to have become well established by the beginning of the 19th century.

Visitors to the famous British landscape painter Joseph Mallord Turner (1775-1851) found him to have seven Manx cats in his studio at Harley Street in London - and he vacated his premises in Harley Street in 1812.

For him to have so many suggests that the Manx cat had become established well before then.

Why, then, no references to them, especially in local newspapers?

The answer, perhaps, lies in indifference.

The first local newspaper, the Manks Mercury, which was established in 1793 wasn't aimed at the native Manx people. Many still spoke only Gaelic and most of those who understood English in which the Mercury was written were illiterate. The paper and others which followed for some years thereafter catered for non-Manx who had settled on the Island because of its low cost of living. Most of the news they carried wasn't about the Island but of elsewhere which concerned these people. What happened locally wasn't of particular concern when the latest "intelligence" concerned the Napoleonic wars.

This tale is NOT "To be continued"!

Myth of the cat-rabbit

In the autumn of 1949 two American families reported finding what they called cat-rabbits. The fronts looked like cats, the rears like rabbits. They disdained milk and one actually liked crunching on a raw potato!

Was it possible, they wondered, that cats had mated with rabbits?

One trapped in Baltimore sat and hopped like a rabbit. Then the Cleveland Plain Dealer reported on another in its area found by Mr and Mrs Paul Beeson of Hartland Avenue, Euclid and called "Rabbit." It was a cat-rabbit, it said...until the telephone lines hummed and letters poured in.

Finally reporter Loveland capitulated. O.K., he said, he'd settle for "Rabbit" being a Manx cat.

One writer, Mrs J. A. Chase, observed: "I'd say 'Rabbit' is just an ordinary Manx cat. Well, maybe not ordinary because nothing from the Isle of Man is ordinary."

Soon-to-be famous for his BBC TV science fiction serials "Quatermass" in the 1950s, Manxman Nigel Kneale weighed in with his own conclusion about the Baltimore find. Surely it was just a Manx cat that had strayed from a Manx family in America? he suggested.

It was an explanation certainly plausible for the location of the second discovery, Cleveland, *was* one of the most popular places for Manx emigrants last century.

For a time, however, there were some who believed the cat-rabbit theory - especially as there was an Isle of Man story to support it. Hadn't cats and rabbits been known to mate there?

In 1937 one of the founders of the Rotary Club movement, biologist Paul Harris, joked about the cats during a visit to the Island with colleagues:

"A gentleman cat fell in love with a lady rabbit, once upon a time," he said. "Their children never knew what they were nor cared. Aft of their mid-scuppers they were rabbit. For'ard they were just cat."

In this he repeated a Victorian myth: that the dark secret of the Manx cat was that it was half cat, half rabbit.

Today geneticists scoff at the idea. But last century many feline-lovers believed it. Reproduced on this page is the reason why - the cat that started the myth.

It's a woodcut print of a Manx cat taken from a drawing in the Isle of Man in August 1837 by Scotsman, Joseph Train of Castle Douglas, Galloway. Later in a book, "An Historical and Statistical Account of the Isle of Man", published in 1845, he revealed his c o n c l u s i o n s (based, he said, on the structure and habits of his own cat).

He had little doubt that it was a mule - a cross between a female cat and a buck rabbit.

"Both in its appearance and habits it differs much from the common house cat," he observed. "The head is smaller in proportion and the body is short; a fud or brush like that of a rabbit, about an inch in length, extending from the lower vertebra, is the only indication it has a tail. The hind legs are considerably longer than those of the common cat and, in comparison with the forelegs, bear a marked similarity in proportion to those of the rabbit.

"Like this animal too, when about to fight, it springs from the ground and strikes with its fore and hind feet at the same time. The common cat strikes only with its fore paws, standing on its hind legs. The rumpy discharges its urine in a standing posture like a rabbit, and can be

carried by the ears, apparently without pain . . ."

Mr Train believed his conclusions to be confirmed by the experiences of John Cunningham of Hensol in the stewartry of Kirkcudbright. A piece of waste land on his estate had been stocked with rabbits which multiplied rapidly, he said; then in the immediate neighbourhood of this warren rumpy cats became plentiful although hitherto they had been unknown in this locality.

"Not a doubt seems to exist as to the nature of this origin," suggested Mr Train.

At the time the argument seemed convincing. But Mr Train had overlooked two important factors.

One: the area was frequented by Manx people. Some even had homes there so probably brought the Island's tailless cats with them.

Two: By providing an abundance of rabbits Mr Cunningham created an excellent food source and hunting ground for Manx cats inclined to stray and go wild.

The great hunting instinct in a Manx was apparent to him; enough for him to comment: "As a mouser the rumpy is preferred to all others of its kind. Formerly when cats were scarce in Europe the rumpy would have brought a high price."

Yet he overlooked rabbits as being a food source! How could he?

The only logical conclusion is that Mr Train was so blinded by his belief that the animal was half-rabbit he couldn't imagine it eating one of its kin.

As for the drawing of the cat (a "monstrosity" some called it), was there *ever* one that looked like that?

The Rev. Theophilus Talbot of Douglas, a keen student of all things Manx in the latter part of the last century, condemned much of Train's book as invention. In a paper given to the Isle of Man Natural History and Antiquarian Society in 1883 he said the woodcut of the cat was well fitted, like Train's verbal description, "to delude innocent readers."

"There can be no doubt that many persons in this Island and especially beyond the seas have formed their notions of tailless cats here from that picture," he said. "But it may be gravely questioned whether a cat with such proportions of height to length (say as 23 to 27) and with a trunk of such a shape, was ever seen by anyone. If meant as a typical form it could scarcely have been better adapted to mislead."

A Manx Cat.

A Manx cat of a different sort – according to cartoonist, Lance Thackeray

The Japanese Connection

(Above) Manx crown of 1994 displays a Japanese Bobtail.

(Below) Two Japanese Bobtail named Chan and Micko.

It looks like a Manx stumpy - but it isn't. It's even on a Manx golden Crown piece. But that's the extent of its Manxness. The cat is a Japanese Bobtail.

From appearances one can understand how there were suspicions at one time that this might have been the originator of the Manx cat or that Manx cats were really Bobtails. The similarities are many.

Indeed, in the 1890s the owner of a Manx stumpy who wanted to enter her cat in a show at London's Crystal Palace was told: Sorry, this wasn't a British cat. She would have to enter it in the 'Foreign' class. Officials were convinced it was Japanese.

It wasn't, of course. But it won the class!

Many Victorians thought the Far East to be the cats' logical origin.

There was the Japanese Bobtail; also the Malay cat in Burma and Siam with a short, sometimes crooked tail.

A writer in the magazine "Science Gossip" in 1865 said a cat with a screw-like knot for a tail was well known in the Burmese empire. A military friend gave him one in Madras and from this quite a family of them developed.

Naturalist Alfred R.Wallace, author of "The Malay Archipelago," suggested in correspondence to a Manxman, E. Birchall, about 1880: "The Malay cat...approaches nearest to the Manx...It seems probable that one or more of these was brought home by some sailor and thus originated the breed. If I remember rightly sometimes the Malay cats have no tail."

Charles Darwin, in his researches into the origins of the species, however, noted significant differences in the Manx cat which distanced it from those in the Far East. There was the greater length of the hind legs, he said; also certain habits.

Manx Government Vet, Douglas Kerruish, added one other difference in the 1960s. The bodies of the other cats were longer and had less depth than a Manx, he said.

Subsequent researchers in the Far East, Russia, Germany and America looked for genetic links but failed to find them. What they established was that the gene for taillessness in Manx cats is different to that elsewhere.

Their conclusion? The Manx is one of nature's accidents...and it happened in the Isle of Man.

The Breed that isn't . . . .

In 1883 after studying Manx cats in their home territory of the Isle of Man for 30 years the Rev Theophilus Talbot claimed: There was no such thing as "a true Manx cat."

He told the Isle of Man Natural History and Antiquarian Society: "No one without extraordinary assumption can point to an individual cat and say: 'That's the normal.'"

There was a diversity in taillessness, he said. Cats differed in length, height, bulk, size of head and body, also in colour and quality of fur.

"The only peculiarity they share in common is taillessness," he declared.

Almost a hundred years later after much scientific research throughout the world into taillessness and a more detailed survey of the resident Manx cat population by a visiting genetics expert from America, Dr Larch Garrad of the Manx Museum and National Trust agreed. There was no such thing as a "pure Manx," she said. All carried the genes to produce a tail. Mate two rumpies and they wouldn't necessarily breed true.

The consequence of this is: the Manx cat isn't a breed, though many think of it as such.

In 1970 at an inter-cities cat show in Ottawa, Canada a Manx cat called Dancing Flame was accepted as an entry in a class for experimental breeds and won it. But that was a mistake. After being around for several hundred years the Manx cat certainly wasn't "experimental" then nor is it a breed. Rather is it what is known as "a variety" of the British shorthaired cat.

Significantly earlier this century the British Shorthaired Cat Society included the words "and Manx Club Incorporated" in its title.

In 1939 the Animal Pictorial reported: "Although the Manx will probably never become a very popular variety they have kept a steady

position in the show world. It is not uncommon for a Manx to get the coveted award of 'Best shorthaired cat in the show.'"

American geneticist Neil Todd, Director of America's Carnivore Genetics Research Centre, was emphatic about it in 1964. "There can be no Manx breed," he told the Montreal Star. "A cat without a tail is no more a special breed than is a man with one and a half or more toes or fingers." As a student at Harvard university he wrote his thesis on taillessness after coming to the Island and taking a Manx kitten back to America for experimental breeding. Thereafter he conducted extensive research on the subject.

"It just so happens," he said, "that the gene which eliminates or stumps cats' tails is much more prevalent among common cats in the Isle of Man than anywhere else in the world." For more than 50 years breeders throughout the world had been trying to produce a pure Manx cat breeding line - all without success, he said.

Isle of Man vet Frank Wadsworth of Ballasalla, however, is one of a number of breeders whose results have contradicted this belief. Ever since the late 1980s his queens Tabatha and Nopur (named such because she didn't purr) have produced perfect rumpies every time.

Feral Manx cats throw tailed and tailless kittens, he suggests, because they mate with different cats.

There are some general similarities in Manxies, however. In March 1930 Dr E. C. Herdman, daughter of the late Sir William Herdman who established Liverpool University's Marine Biological Station at Port Erin, revealed the results of studies she had undertaken at the university. She listed the following characteristics:

* A short broad back, sloping upwards;

This small souvenir dish produced by Goss China depicts a brown Manx cat taken from a print used on souvenirs from the 1870s. On the opposite page the same print is incorporated in one of the earliest postcards produced on the Isle of Man in about 1900. The writer says "The little maid says she will buy the cat a new tail."

* Long hind legs which give a "jumpy kind of progression";

* A heavier pelvis than normal cats; and

* A lack of responsiveness in the tail region. Stroke it there, she said, and it shouldn't make an effort to respond.

In 1907 *the* Isle of Man Times complained that show judges outside the Island knew nothing of the Manx cat's history or peculiarities. A Manx Cat Society (now defunct) confessed: People had different ideas as to what constituted an ideal Manx. Thirty years later an Isle of Man judge confessed that differences of opinion existed still.

The first known show specification for a Manx was published in 1889 by Harrison Weir FRHS, president of Britain's National Cat Club.

In a booklet "The Standard for Points of Excellence and Beauty," he said the heads of Manx cats should be small; yet today the requirement is for one larger than the average British cat.

Fur should be short, of even length, "smooth, silky and glossy," he said. It should lie close to the body, be bright and full of lustre. There was no mention of the double coat and rabbity feel which are known to be special features.

Later a Manx Cat Society official ventured the opinion that a squat "pudding" specimen should never win a show prize. The Manx cat was naturally a lithe, acrobatic animal. Her specification was: strongly built, short back and high hind legs; lengthy nose with cut-away cheeks, ears large at the base with pronounced points and good breadth

of skull between them; coat, close and "rabbity." Cats with short, silky coats should be debarred from shows, she said, as being crosses with British shorthaired cats.

American show judges have allocated points for Manxness on various scales, taillessness consistently accounting for only 15 points out of a maximum 100. At one stage height and hind quarters accounted for 15 points, shortness of back, 15; roundness of rump, 10; depth of flank, 10; the coat, 10; head and ears, 10; colour and markings, 5; eyes, 5 and condition, 5. Later the marking was changed to: head and ears, 25; body, 25; taillessness, 15; legs and feet, 15, coat, 10, eyes, 5; colour and markings, 5.

In 1953 when a short-lived Manx Cat Association was established on the Isle of Man it produced a judging standard which allocated 45 per cent of the marks to the degree of taillessness and height of the hindquarters and 40 per cent for roundness of the rump, depth of flank, shape of head and ears and the quality of the coat. The colour of coat and eyes was dismissed as being irrelevant.

How *big* should a Manx cat be? Many Isle of Man cat lovers think it irrelevant.

In the U.S.A. breeders have produced rumpies at both extremes - large and small. Some queens have been reported as being so small they have been unable to deliver kittens naturally and have had to have Caesareans.

The east coast has tended to favour small cats (between six and

14lbs); the west coast much larger rumpies. One - a big, easy-going, typical old-fashioned Manx called Canyon Rim Mannanan Mac Lir - reached up to 25lbs in his prime. He had a reputation for producing few defective kittens.

In America it has been claimed that some breeders have force-fed their cats with a tube to make them gain weight but that is scarcely a natural condition.

In the Isle of Man Manx cats of all sizes have been known. One pedigree breeder, Mary Hughes whose cattery of Vaghee Rossty, is based at East Foxdale has detected a tendency to miniaturisation - caused, she believes, by inbreeding.

Some kittens have been called "hoppers" because that is how they get about, especially when in a hurry

or excited. Good specimens can walk normally, however, if they wish. Rumpies with exaggerated hops are usually subject to an excessive deformity in the spine which renders their rear legs unable to function independent of each other.

Occasionally Manx kittens are born with rear legs the wrong way round. For them nothing can be done but fortunately the problem is rare.

Hind legs should be heavy-boned and sufficiently long to raise the rump slightly higher than the shoulders. Writing about it in 1861, Dr George Wilson said this meant that Manx cats weren't as graceful in movement as others but they were better leapers. At birth there is a tendency for kittens to drag their hind legs flat on the ground behind them until they have developed some strength in them. Front legs should be much shorter but not so severe as

to exaggerate the difference between front and back.

Last century one Manx cat in the Isle of Man was reported to have front legs so short that they were useless for walking. The cat sat up like a kangaroo. But that was a disability, not a guide to perfection.

Equally it should be stressed that a Manx cat *does* have four legs. A Chicago newspaper said once that prized Manxies were the three-legged type. These had actually inspired the Island's Three Legs emblem but this was pure fiction.

In 1951 a three legged tabby known as Tibby was owned by Mr J. M. Coole of Kilkenny, Braddan. The missing leg was the front right. A few years later a grey-blue rumpy was born in and roamed the Hillside Avenue area of Douglas with only three legs - two back and one in the centre of its chest. Some might have considered these appropriate as Manxies considering that the Island's traditional emblem is Three Legs. Certainly in the more gullible Victorian and Edwardian eras they would have been displayed as 'true' Manx. A three-legged dog - Prince Toby Orry - who had lost a front leg in an accident with a Douglas cable car, was promoted so much as being the last of a rare breed which had inspired the Island's Three Legs symbol that china models of him were sold to tourists.

The truth, however, is that both the kangaroo and three-legged Manxies were rare malformations.

Occasionally Manx cats are born with more than the average number of toes: five on the front paws, four on the rear. They are known as Polydactyl which means "many digits." Among the superstitious it has been claimed that ownership of one implies witchcraft!

Odin, a magnificent ginger tom with white chest and white paws who was the principal breeding tom at the Manx Cattery immediately prior to its closure, had six toes on every paw.

Some feral kittens found near Douglas Gas Works on the South Quay in Douglas and given to the Ellan Vannin Cat Protection Trust, established in the early 1990s to run a cat sanctuary and help alleviate suffering among cats, were found to have seven toes. One had an extra thumb on which were the buds of more toes. Initially the kittens didn't seem handicapped by this; however Laurel Collis of Kirk Michael, one of the Trust's four trustees who kept one of the kittens, a ginger male, discovered a long term problem. Some of the extra claws didn't touch the ground so weren't subject to normal wear. This meant regular cutting of the claws to prevent them becoming overlong.

According to former Manx Government Vet Douglas Kerruish, the coats of Manx cats should be double: a distinct undercoat with a harder top coat.

Long-haired tailless cats started to appear in American cat shows in the late sixties and early seventies. They became known as Cymric. In 1963 they were claimed on

YES DEAR, BY RIGHTS I AM THE DUKE OF PORTLAND!

THE MANX CATS HAVE NO TAILS!

BUT THE JOHNNIES THERE CAN TELL EM ALRIGHT!

the Isle of Man to be a hybrid between short-haired Manx and Persians and the result of three years of breeding and research by an associate member of the Manx Fanciers Association in America, Mrs Carol Oakham of California. When the cats first appeared some breeders said they intended to oppose their recognition as Manx cats. Subsequently, however, it was claimed that Cymrics were the result of breeding two long-haired Manx together.

Sylvia Church of Orpington, Kent has included in one of the pedigrees she received from the Manx Cattery, the description "shaggy Manx." She believes this to be a local description of the long-haired cat.

The gene for long fur, she theorises, was brought to the Island from Norway when the Vikings conquered the Isle of Man. Centuries later when the Manx cat mutation occurred some inherited the gene for long fur too.

Only one long-haired cat is believed to have been known at the Manx Cattery. That was Izzy. Both his mother and father had short fur but apparently his mother carried the gene for longer fur as she gave birth to several more long-furred kittens later.

According to oral tradition in their native homeland the "true" Manx cat is a tabby of which there are three types: a "Blotched" which has large circular black markings, a "Mackerel" because the distinctive stripes resemble fish bones and the third, "Spotted," because of the resemblance of the markings to black

spots. The distinctive "M" in black fur above the top of the nose stands for "Manx."

Today the story is dismissed by breeders as an invention of the Victorian Manx.

Whilst it is true that a great many early 20th century photographs and drawings of Manx cats on the Island depicted them as being tabby, "lucky black Manxies" were being sold to tourists and displayed on souvenir china ware.

The truth is that Manx cats come in all colours and combinations of them, even those of a Persian. The fact that many early Isle of Man photographs and drawings depict them as tabbies suggests a sub-conscious preference on the Island for them.

In 1942 veteran Isle of Man cat show judge, Mr A. Teare of Ballaugh, said the most popular colour locally was brown with black markings and no white anywhere. Often this was known as tiger.

A survey in the late 1970s revealed that ginger was a predominantly male

colour. Dr Larch Garrad of the Manx Museum called it "the genetic norm." A ginger female born in July 1980 at the Kirby Garden Centre was reckoned to be "one in 26,000," and was probably sterile.

When the Government Cattery was established at Knockaloe and

then later at Noble's Park the operators found that American buyers were particulary choosy over colour. Most didn't like cats with patches of white. They wanted "solid" colours: all black, all white, all ginger and so on: not easy to satisfy.

Pure white Manx cats are scarce but not as much as sometimes claimed.

In 1952 a prizewinning pure white rumpy known as "Snowy Guilder Rose," owned by Mrs Ann Vaughan of Liscard, Wallasey, was claimed by the Sunday Express to be the only pure white Manx cat in the world.

Manx people were quick to deny it. Cats with the names of "Snowy" and "Snowball" were produced as proof. One owned by local breeder Jessie Twining of Greeba had won the award for best Manx cat at the Isle of Man's Fur and Feather Show in 1951.

Nevertheless "Snowy Guilder Rose" was exhibited at a Festival of Cats in London in August 1952, described then as "believed to be the only pure white Manx cat in the country."

The rarity of pure white rumpies was demonstrated when the Manx Government Cattery at Knockaloe tried to breed them. It did so for years without any notable success.

Hence the amazement when two undistinguished mackerel-tabbies at Peel produced four flawless all-white rumpies in one litter in January 1971. Their owner, Mrs Ivy Quirk of Station Road, Peel was told by Cattery supervisor, Mrs Violet Holroyd: They were kittens in a million, a wonderful "throw-back" to a past generation.

Blue Manx are rare, particularly on the Isle of Man. When Freda Williams of the Dreemskerry Manx Cattery in Hampshire first established her Cattery she advertised for two years for a blue queen. Eventually a woman in Tromode, Isle of Man who had two pet females responded and Freda bought one.

In 1963 she received an offer of £50 for Grey Dawn from the Manx Cattery at Knockaloe. It was a lot for a cat, she said, but she didn't sell and ever since has been glad she didn't for from that one kitten she believes most of the Manx blues in England and abroad have originated.

Since the early 1990s Manx cats with perfect Persian markings have been bred by Mary Hughes of East Foxdale, for 22 years a breeder of Persian cats. The breeding of pedigree Colour Point Manx was reported also in New Zealand.

Mrs Hughes became interested in Manx in about 1986 when serving as a veterinary nurse with a local vet. One day some three-week old kittens were brought in to be put down. They had been found in a greenhouse and no one wanted them. The vet decided to find good homes for them and did so. Mrs Hughes adopted one, a black female rumpy which she called Curragh Fem.

The rumpy was crossed with a Colour Point Persian bred by Mrs Hughes and this led to the development of a pedigree line of Colour Point Manx; body shape and taillessness, all Manx, the colour that of a Persian. Mrs Hughes said she hoped that by introducing new colours into the variety there would be greater world interest in it.

The only lilac Manx registered in Britain in 1995 was believed to be Yched Nane (Manx for 'First One'), also bred by Mrs Hughes. The grandfather was Persian.

Manx Government Vet Douglas Kerruish, reckoned that show judges liked the heads of Manx cats to be larger than British shorthaired cats, round with no tendency to "snipyness." Ears should be wide at the base tapering to a point.

Veteran show judge in the 1920s, '30s and '40s, Mr A. Teare of Ballaugh, Isle of Man believed the nose should be longer than a good British shorthair and the cheeks should be prominent.

In the U.S.A. some breeders and show judges have encouraged "jowliness" about the face, especially for males.

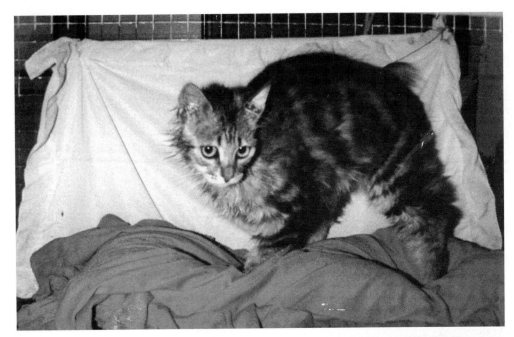

The only "shaggy cat" Manx cat born at the Manx Cattery: young "Izzy" after having his ears syringed.

A Midwood card, Douglas

PRIZE WHITE MANX KITTENS.

Breeder & Exhibitor
J·K·CURPHEY·

"Laxey"
Regd. No B4807.

"Port Erin"
Regd. No B4806.

9705   "A MANX BEAUTY"   ROTARY PHOTO. E.C.

One of the most popular eye colours among American breeders and show judges is copper. According to Mr Kerruish, however, native Manx cats usually had yellow or greenish eyes. Orange was considered desirable by some but it was unusual, therefore probably attributable to the introduction into the breed of "foreign" blood. Breeder, Sylvia Church of Orpington, Kent believes green to be the predominant colour.

Occasionally some cats are born with odd coloured eyes. A pure white rumpy in Ballaugh known as Popeye had one blue and one green eye; another had one blue and one yellow.

One prominent British breeder in 1923, Will Hally, had what he described as "two of the finest white Manx" he had seen yet the colour of their eyes meant that show judges didn't give them the recognition Mr Hally believed they deserved. The problem lay in their eyes. White cats should have blue eyes, they said. These cats had orange. As a result, show judges wouldn't accept the cats: a curious ruling in the light of modern developments where animal right activists campaign against the deliberate breeding of blue-eyed white cats because of a tendency for them to be deaf. A case now of: Better to be orange-

Proof of the uncertainty of a Manx cat's offspring: here's a tabby with her pure-white kittens.

Carran and Kathy – two Manx kittens at eleven weeks. They were born in Holland on 17th May 1994.

eyed and of good hearing than blue-eyed and deaf?

Isle of Man judge, Mr Teare of Ballaugh, thought eye colour to be of little importance. It should be taken into account, he said, only when structural points between cats were equal.

Rumps are an important feature. They should be "round like an orange," said prominent breeder Will Hally in 1923. He considered narrow, pointed rumps "one of the worst faults that a Manx can have."

Manx cats can be very independent-minded, determined and prone to go wild in the Isle of Man - yet they are affectionate too.

Writer Aldous Huxley claimed once that as a tail is a cat's principal organ of emotional expression, a rumpy's inability to communicate with one like other cats makes it like a dumb man, unable to express itself. But that's not true.

Manx cats can be very expressive.

Breeder, Mary Hughes, has noted a tendency for the fur at a Manx cat's rear to rise perceptively as a sign of pleasure.

Helen Hill Shaw of Croyden, Surrey - secretary of Britain's Manx Cat Club in 1933 - wrote then: "It was my privilege on one occasion to witness the reunion of a Manx cat and his loved mistress from whom he had been parted for over four years during her stay in Africa. His joy was most touching; he recognised her at once, jumping on her knee and shoulder and kissing her repeatedly, refusing to be separated from her again."

Manx cats can be quite courageous - "tough-spirited," as Judy Corrin of Foxdale, a qualified veterinary nurse and Animal Welfare Officer for the Manx Society for the Prevention of Cruelty to Animals, puts it. One of her farm cats, Aalish (Manx for Alice), intervened between dog fights on a number of occasions. "She just jumped in, claws out and hissing and the dogs parted," she said. "She's run the whole length of a garden to split them up."

Sylvia Church has seen one of her cats, Tabatha, walk up to an alsation and "wack it across the face."

Sally Black of Castletown remembers her Manx cat, Ramsey, born in Charlottesville, Virginia, squaring up to a four-foot round-bodied black snake which reared menacingly several feet into the air. Unperturbed, Ramsey stood his ground on top of a tree stump and batted it with his paws until the snake decided it wasn't going to win this particular encounter and retired.

Laurel Collis of the Ellan Vannin Cat Protection Trust can testify to the toughness of Manx cats.

In 1994 a feral stumpy tabby began lingering about her remote farm at Kirk Michael, evidently looking for food. At first whenever someone approached him he would run off and hide but eventually he was coaxed into the farmhouse. Laurel detected a terrible smell as he

I'm Manx!   Who are you?   I'm English!

walked into the porch and settled in a dog basket. Later, when she had won sufficient trust to examine him, she found that all four paws were covered in a material which had been molten at some stage and then had solidified. Beneath it the cat's paws were putrefying.

"I don't know how he had managed to walk," said Laurel later. "He was in a terrible mess."

Fortunately a vet was able to remove the plastic-like substance without causing too much damage to the underlying paws and the cat slowly responded to loving care. Laurel gave him the name of Perick, Manx for Patrick - "because he had the luck of the Irish in coming to me," she said.

Freda Williams of Dreemskerry Manx Cattery in Hampshire has found Manx cats to be exceptionally trustworthy.

On one occasion she and a companion motored across America with 17 Manx cats and 28 racing pigeons all loose together in a truck. "Not a bird was touched," she said. "What other cat could you train to be like that?"

"Dog-like" is another attribute. Sometimes a Manx can be trained to retrieve small balls; even to walk in harness. A special Manx cat harness was developed by Freda Williams some years ago.

Sylvia Church has walked her cats round the shopping centre in her home town. "It takes only ten minutes or so to teach them to walk on the lead," she says.

A feral cat colony established on rocks overlooking the Douglas Horse Tram stables in the 1950s and composed mostly of Manx cats descended from ones that had lived in the stables used to let a toy poodle join in their games. Sadly their trust in dogs was misplaced. In January 1958 two were caught by a dog and killed.

The cry of the Manx cat is usually more shriller than most other cats. Females in season utter a guttural sound. They can be talkative too.

Water provides few fears. Edwardian comic postcards even depicted rumpies swimming.

The truth is: Many Manx cats seem fascinated by water.

Mrs Sheila Quaggin of Douglas, formerly one of the staff at the Manx Cattery, discovered to her surprise that some actually liked to play in the spray when the Cattery was being hosed down. Others liked to sit by the sink.

In the wild, some will even swim after prey! A survey on cat prey undertaken by Dr Larch Garrad of the Manx Museum included trout.

Jane Hellman of Tattleberry Manx in Dyfed, Wales once had a rumpy who plunged into a pond after a moorhen and caught it.

Judy Corrin of Foxdale had a tabby kitten called Willow who loved to join her

Time is flying (it struck me in the flight),
I've nothing of a "tale" but hope you keep all right.

The Seaside Smile in Manxland.

in the bath. Later the cat took to swimming a few minutes at a time in the farm pond - just for the love of it.

Sylvia Church's stud tom "Dhoolish," loved to join her in the bath. Unafraid of water, he jumped onto her stomach and pawed at the bubbles she made for him.

Mrs Quaggin had two which liked to sit on the side of the bath when her husband was in it. They flicked the water and washed themselves with it.

Manx Cats are good ratters and rabbiters. In the Isle of Man they have been known to catch seagulls; in the U.S., gophers too.

Because they have no tails some people think they lack a normal cat's balancing powers and can't climb but that's not so. Douglas breeder, Mrs Sheila Quaggin, believes the large, powerful hind legs compensate.

Manxies are good climbers and sometimes are not averse to letting this ability be used by others. One cat owned by Sylvia Church used to climb apple trees and shake the branches to dislodge apples for a dog below who was particularly partial to them.

The climbing abilities of

Tuppence, a Manx cat owned by British Railways clerk Ted Livesey, won him an award in 1948. Tuppence climbed a rose arch at the bottom of Ted's garden and looked so magnificent among the blooms that he photographed her there. Later his picture won first prize in a photographic competition organised by the western region of British Railways staff association.

Eddie Hallam, owner for 25 years of the Riber Trust Fauna Reserve (now under different ownership and known as the Riber Castle Wild Life Park, set in 25 acres of land around a ruined castle at Matlock, Derby) can testify to the Manx cat's hunting abilities. In 1964 and the following year he acquired three Manx cats from the Cattery in the Isle of Man and let them roam round his grounds. One of them, a predominantly white tom with grey-blue markings, proved to be "the most fantastic mouser and ratter I have ever known," he said later. "It

was absolutely incredible. I've seen it get two rats in a fraction of a second, dragging one along with it as it went after the other."

Such hunting abilities, however, can have its disadvantages. Breeders in the Isle of Man who let their cats roam the countryside have reported losses due to poisoning. The suspicion is that rat poison has been transferred down the food chain.

Eddie lost his top cat because of rats - but not through poison, rather a disease known as Leptospirosis spread by rat urine. That, he has suggested, is more likely to be the explanation for deaths of good hunters elsewhere. If cats bite into and puncture a rat's bladder then the urine can spread the infection.

A favourite hunting tactic of Manx cats in the Isle of Man is to sit on a hedge overlooking the entrance to a rabbit burrow, preferably a nest hole, then pounce on an emerging rabbit.

"Big Ginge" from the Manx Cattery being playful and inquisitive. Note legs and rump.

Good hunters though they are, Manx cats can show respect for natural prey that are close to home.

Brian and Sheila Waiting of Ballavolley Lodge, Ballaugh have known their cats return home after hunting expeditions in the boggy Curragh nearby with two or three pheasant a day and some ducks and duckling - yet never touch the "pet" ducks at home. Indeed, the cats have played and fed with those ducks, apparently accepting them as family.

A similar experience occurred to Mary Corkish of Ballawattleworth dairy farm. One day she hatched out a motherless gosling and placed it in the bottom oven of her Aga cooker to keep warm. A little later she was surprised to see the gosling snuggling up to one of her working farm cats, Snowy, a pure white Manx.

Like the rest of her farm cats he was kept as a hunter to keep rats at bay (the birth of Manxies and their sale abroad was just incidental). Yet here he "adopted" the gosling and in the weeks that followed he helped rear it.

At the Dhoon-based Rhenab Poultry Farm in the summer of 1948, a cat called Tiger had two kittens then roamed the fields on a hunting expedition. She returned with a live, unharmed black baby rabbit which she carried by the neck into the farm's kitchen where the kittens were and to the astonishment of farmers, Mr and Mrs J. W. Reid, she placed the rabbit with her small litter and proceeded to raise it as one of her own. Later she brought back another rabbit, this time a grey one, but Mr and Mrs Reid returned that one to the wild. One rabbit roaming their home was enough, they thought.

As the rabbit matured the farm cats, all good hunters, accepted him as "family." They even let him play with them. He, in turn, had some influence on how the kittens behaved. They were seen to nibble at the rabbit's lettuce leaves!

Kipper, a pure black rumpy which roamed at will for more than 13 years in the Manx Government-owned Wild Life Park at Ballaugh, had a reputation for ignoring the local bird life.

The explanation, however, isn't always a bonding between animals as "family." Sometimes it can be the result of a healthy respect for what birds can do.

A 13 year old cockatoo owned by Sylvia Church in Kent and known as George Michael gained the upper hand one day after her cats knocked over his cage. He bit their paws.

Thereafter the cats avoided the cockatoo.

Such is the Manx cat's reputation as a hunter that when Manxman Leslie Dibb arrived in the island of Orkney during his military service in the Second World War he was asked: Please could he get the islanders some Manx cats? The island was overrun by rats but they had heard that rumpies were excellent at killing them, better than other cats. So eager were they to introduce rumpies into the island they offered Mr Dibb free butter and cheese for the rest of the war: a substantial incentive in those difficult times.

Mr Dibb wasn't able to satisfy the

needs of Orkney because of pressure on his time and transport problems during wartime. However, the fact that he received such an approach indicated the reputation of the Manx cat as a hunter.

Famous British band leader, composer and pianist Ronnie Aldrich of The Squadronnaires who had his home in the Isle of Man overlooking the sea at Port St Mary for almost 30 years prior to his death in 1993 was astonished once when he saw his three year old pure black stumpy, Mona, catch a bat.

"We couldn't believe it," said his wife Mary later. "It was early dusk and two or three bats were flitting about, swooping down for insects. We were looking idly into the garden when we saw Mona leap suddenly into the air and end up on the ground with a bat between her paws. What a spring it must have been! We have a high stone garden wall, about ten feet, and her leap must have been near half that height."

Mona ate the bat as if it was a mouse.

Another ability demonstrated by Manxies is a good 'homing' instinct.

In 1957 two-year-old Bunty became known as the cat with "radar on his whiskers."

The previous December he had been taken from his home in Patrick to live in Douglas with Miss Mona Chilcot of 8 Spring Gardens. He had been transported all the way by car and had slept in transit so had no way of knowing his way back.

The lofty plunge is our daily joy,
    And other aquatic pranks;
Though we've many a tale,
Our "stern sheets"   do fail,
    Because we are   cats of the Manx.

Kys ta Shiu?

When he went missing six days later, therefore, and severe blizzards blocked roads it was feared he was lost.

Twenty-five days after vanishing, however, Bunty arrived back at Patrick looking none the worse for his experience. How he had managed it no one could explain.

No doubt the basic instinct to go wild had seen him through.

A similar experience befell Ballaugh-based breeders for 25 years Sheila and Brian Waiting. About 45 minutes after a couple who lived several miles away had collected by car a nine month old smokey grey cat called Fluffy from them they received news by telephone that Fluffy had escaped from her new home and had disappeared.

Mr and Mrs Waiting went to the house, rattled tins and boxes in the hope that Fluffy would respond to them but there was no sign of her.

Four days later though when Mrs Waiting was in the kitchen doing some ironing she heard miaowing at the backdoor and there was Fluffy, none the worse for being at large.

This time Fluffy's new owners kept her securely indoors for a month and thereafter there were no problems.

Reports vary according to litter sizes. Brian and Sheila Waiting reported nine kittens in one litter (one born dead and one dead soon after) and wondered if it was a record. However, in the 1880s the Rev Theophilus

Talbot of Douglas recorded one litter of a dozen.

The normal litter, however, is usually between four and five.

The ratio of tailless to tailed kittens in litters varies widely. Some breeders have reported a ratio of three tailed to one rumpy; some "half and half," others that they get tailless every time. Last century the Rev Talbot said that sometimes in large litters there could be only one tailless kitten.

The tendency in the U.S.A. for some breeders to produce very small Manx cats means that sometimes queens are unable to give birth naturally and have to be given caesareans. This is not normal in the Isle of Man.

As with humans the life expectancy of a Manx cat depends on each individual case.

Judy Corrin had a neutered male called Skeet who lived to be 15. Ballasalla vet Frank Wadsworth knows of one who lived to be 19.

Manx historian Mona Douglas reported in 1971 that a cat owned by Miss May Teare of Marathon Road, Douglas and called Kirry lived into her 20s. Her exact age was unknown because she was a stray. A pregnant Kirry arrived on Miss Teare's small verandah one night mewing so pitifully that Miss Teare gave her a home and found homes for all her kittens too.

Kirry became known as "The T.V. Cat" because of her appearance on BBC television in the 1950s. A local folk singer, Joan Owen, was to appear on a live broadcast from Wales. She wanted to be accompanied by a Manx cat so Miss Teare let Kirry go along.

A brindle tortoiseshell called Cowin who lived in Castle Mona Avenue, Douglas died in 1970 aged 22.

The record for a Manx seems to be held, however, by a 23 year old called Mitzie, owned by a man in Buffalo, New York. In December 1951 he gave his recipe for her longevity as a daily diet of greens, shrimps, lobster tail, beef steak, liver and the cream of rich milk.

The secret for longevity? Look after your cat!

Said Mona Douglas after losing a tailed cat which lived to be 28: "Too many people think that cats can look after themselves."

FIRST ADDITION
GREETINGS FROM ELLAN VANNIN.

I am Pussy, little Pussy,
With my fur so close and glossy,
I'm the Pride of Mona surely,
Now the same as days of yore;
Though I ate the fat canary,
Yet the rats I've chased from dairy,
And ten thousand mice I've killed before to-day.

I cannot come to see you
But I'll always be at home,
If you'll come across the briny
Throughout the Isle we'll roam:
I'll show you all the beauty spots
Of mountain, glen, and dale,
And prove to you, beyond a doubt,
That Three Legs is really nought
When placed beside No Tail.

QUEEN MAB

 Now I claim to be the oldest, and possibly the boldest,
Of pioneers who first arrived on Man;
Though the Three-Legged Doggies boast of an ancestry remote,
They can't produce the evidence I can.

A2 Copyright. E.M. Reg. 54. No. 57,865.

"Queen Mab" was a popular Manx tabby on Edwardian postcards. The sender of this one posted in July 1913, wrote: "Would you like a young Queen Mab? The Manx cats are not as plentiful as they were".

"Yes Dear, we spent our holiday in the
Isle of Man last year!"

Posing and Pottery

It's the distinctive Manx cat pose on a racing motorcycle - American style!

Exaggerated, perhaps - but it emphasises one of the most dominant characteristics of many Manx cats: the tendency for the rump or part of its back to be raised higher than its neck.

The pottery models of black and white cats on the previous page, produced in about the same era for sale as tourist souvenirs, support the pose as being that of a Manx cat.

Not all rumpies display this characteristic, however, as the illustration of the tabby on the left of the page illustrates. This particular cat was used on many Manx postcards at the turn of the century but neither his back nor the height of his rump conformed with the accepted body structure.

This demonstrates how variable the tailless cat can be on the Isle of Man and how little importance many Manx people attached then to body shape. All that mattered was taillessness.

It *was* in 1911 that cartoonist John Bryan noted the similarity between the racing style and that of a "true" Manx cat. He imagined shepherds on Manx hillsides being terrified by some monster rumpy emerging out of the morning mists, roaring and spitting flame.

The style became known as "Jaking" after American dirt track champion Jake de Rosier. He demonstrated it in the Isle of Man on a red-painted American Indian machine. That was the year when the

world famous T.T. international motorcycle road race adopted the equally famous 37.75 mile Snaefell mountain course for the first time. Wearing figure-hugging theatrical tights astride a bright red factory-entered Indian Jake's riding style astonished spectators.

The style wasn't as eccentric as it first appeared, though. The roads were so rutted and bumpy that many riders suffered badly from prolonged juddering. By adopting the Manx cat pose and keeping his rear end in the air over the worst parts of the course Jake reduced the jarring to his body.

Few other breeds or varieties of cat have had as many pottery and china models made of them as the Manx.

Ever since mid-Victorian times the cat has been the subject of innumerable items of souvenir ware, many white, a few black, some with transfer prints of local coats of arms on their sides.

Not all are a reliable guide, however, to the physical shape and proportions of a Manx cat. The models haven't been of Manx cats at all. Manufacturers have merely made them from moulds of normal British shorthairs and chopped off their tails!

Local potters have produced a number of model cats since the early sixties.

In May 1964 when the now defunct Ramsey Pottery was opened on the corner of the market square and the quay one of its range was a glazed Manx cat. Managing director Clarence Pinel said it was modelled on his own seven-month old cat called Prow Prow, winner of three trophies at local shows. Unfortunately Prow Prow couldn't make it to the official opening of the Pottery. She had a prior engagement - the arrival of a litter of kittens!

Shebeg Gallery, established by John Harper on the Ballamodha Straight in the spring of 1968, became internationally famous for the production for breed societies of models of pedigree cattle but occasionally its range of models included Manx cats, designed from personal observation of cats on the Island and official breed descriptions. In about 1970 models were produced of a semi-porcelain cat about four and a half inches high, some black, others white, tortoisehell and tabby. Subsequent cats were made of porcelain. They included large numbers of a popular two inch high green eyed white cat, produced in 1982. Why green eyes, not blue? "I just thought it looked nice," he said.

Three limited editions, each of 50, have been produced since of six inch models: one in 1987, another (all black), in 1990 and a black and white one in 1995.

Rushton Ceramics, established by John Liddle at the Jurby Industrial Estate in 1973 and based later at the Tynwald Craft Centre at St John's, has produced four types of cat in white earthenware - one small, one medium size and two six inch models, one standing and one sitting. Popular colours have proved to be orange, tabby, grey and black; the tabby and black the most popular of all.

In 1995 a new range of Manx cats in black and white, tabby and tortoisehell, mounted on wooden plinths, were produced by Scotland's Treviotdale Design Co., Ltd., based at Harwick, The Borders. They were for sale exclusively at the Ramsey Gallery in Market Hill, Ramsey.

The mythical rosy-cheeked three legged Manxman in top hat and red coat was a popular tourist souvenir in Victorian and Edwardian times. Always he appeared with his black rumpy cat, the latter sat on an outstretched foot. Many of the china souvenirs were made in Bohemia.

Gifts for the Rich and Famous

One day in January 1978 a white chested Manx cat called Cheeky departed from Peel in the Isle of Man for Los Angeles, U.S.A.

The intended recipient was film star John Wayne.

Cheeky was the gift of Peel Town Commissioner Harry Faragher of Ballafaragher, Market Street, Peel, a retired member of the Manchester Constabulary.

Whilst he was a police officer on an exchange visit to the L.A. police department some years earlier Mr Faragher met John Wayne and was told by him that he had never seen a Manx cat.

Mr Faragher remembered that when his cat Chi-Chi had two rumpy kittens in November 1977. Here was a chance to let John Wayne not only see a Manx cat but have one.

Friends visiting the Isle of Man from Los Angeles agreed to take the kitten back with them.

Thus one more Manx cat emigrated as a gift.

The policy of giving rumpies as presents from the Island has been an on-going private and public activity for at least a century. The cats have been considered outstanding ambassadors of the Isle of Man, stimulating awareness of the Island among people who would otherwise never have heard of the place.

In 1969, for example, Manx Government Vet Bob Hawkins met Swedish writer Dr Magdalen Lagermann whilst holidaying in Almunecar in Spain. As a result he sent a Manx cat to him the following year. Dr Lagermann called the cat Almunecar Douglas, entered it in Sweden's national cat show at Stockholm and it won the supreme championship.

In Australia in 1983 the recipient of a cat gift was the Governor of Victoria. Felix Gratis was the gift of a resident Manxman, Major Max

Crellin, who had the cat's brother, known as "T.T."

After a year Felix was reported to have grown into "a big feather-cushion type cat."

Probably the most prolific distributor of Manx cats was the moustachioed George Cave of the Walpole Private Hotel in Walpole Avenue, Douglas.

During the First World War whilst serving in the Sherwood Foresters he was First Orderly to General Seely in France. Later, as a reminder of their time together, George sent the General a Manx kitten. So began a lifetime's interest.

Nottingham-born George first came to the Island to live when a young man in need of somewhere to convalesce after an illness. With him he brought his pet dogs, three poms. By the time he was fit, however, and had a job as a richly-uniformed porter at the white-painted castellated Fort Anne Hotel on Douglas Head - once one of the top hotels on the Island but now demolished - he had become hooked on Manx cats. He started breeding them at the hotel and eventually became known as "probably the greatest living authority on the tailless cat."

At the hotel George met the rich and famous. When they expressed interest in Manx cats he was quick to supply them, all house trained by the use of kipper boxes as litter trays. Sir Harry Lauder, the entertainer, received an all black rumpy.

For more than thirty years Mr Cave exported hundreds of rumpies; one of

DIGNITY AND IMPUDENCE!

Hi, Kelly!

his most unusual customers was a London monastery. Some he bred himself; others he acquired from Manx people who knew of his interest.

"I don't go about with my eyes shut," he said once. "It's surprising the number of rumpies there are in Douglas. I pick them up here and there for half a crown (twelve and a half new pence) or five bob (25p)..." Sometimes he was given them for nothing, he said.

By the 1930s Mr Cave was known as "The Manx Cat King."

"It's not a commercial matter," he said. There was "nowt in it" for him. "It's just good publicity for the Island to get Manx kittens into the homes of prominent people in different parts of the world."

In 1934 Lady Alexandra Haig, daughter of First World War hero the late Field Marshal Earl Haig, received a Manx kitten at Ramsey whilst visiting the Island as a guest of the Isle of Man branch of the British Legion. She took it back with her to her home in Scotland.

Mr Cave considered his greatest honour, however, to be the receipt of a request on behalf of the Prince of Wales to supply a rumpy for the prince's farm in Nottingham. Mr Cave despatched what he called "a real beauty."

In the late 1920s rumpies were sent to the chief station masters of every main railway station in London. Mr Cave's theory: As the cats wandered the stations their taillessness would attract attention and remind people of the Isle of Man.

Queen Elizabeth 11 very nearly had a Manx cat as a childhood pet.

One was offered but was declined by her mother who feared setting a precedent for other pets to be offered.

Princess Elizabeth was only six years old when the offer was made. An uncle on her father's side, Prince George, was to visit the Isle of Man in June 1932 and it was suggested that perhaps he could take a Manx kitten back for the princess.

Official enquiries were made with her mother (the future Queen Mother, then Duchess of York) as to whether such a gift would be acceptable but after much consideration she said the kitten couldn't be accepted for fear of creating a precedent.

"It appears that the only pet the princess is allowed to have is a canary," said one of the Manx government team responsible for the offer, "and only that because it was a gift from a member of the royal family."

Prince George received a kitten during his visit nevertheless...for himself. Whilst visiting Castletown to turn on a new brew at Castletown Brewery he was presented with a black Manx kitten "for luck" by Miss Eliza Bridson of Ballabeg. It was given to him in a box with cotton wool as packing and after some admiring glances he had it sent to Government House for him to collect later.

In July 1945 Princess Elizabeth and her younger sister Princess Margaret almost received a Manx kitten after all.

It happened when King George VI became the first British monarch to preside at a sitting of Tynwald at St John's.

Both King George and Queen Elizabeth stayed at Government House and the occasion was less formal than would be usual: more a family occasion for Countess Granville, wife of the Island's Lt-Governor, was the sister of Queen Elizabeth.

To add to the atmosphere of an evening dinner the Lt-Governor borrowed a young Manx cat from a member of staff and allowed it to meander round the room. Suddenly, to everyone's surprise, it took a flying leap onto the royal lap then dodged across the dining table. When footmen tried to remove it, the cat dug its claws into the table cloth then scampered among the plates and glasses.

Only one person was amused. That was the king. He "thoroughly enjoyed the incident," claimed a Manx reporter many years later. After the meal King George played with the cat for some time and eventually it was suggested: Perhaps he and the queen would like to take it back to Buckingham Palace? They could give it as a pet to Princess Elizabeth and Princess Margaret.

Briefly, it seems, the royal couple were tempted. This would be a family gift after all, not an official one that could set precedents. Then King George said the cat might not be very happy with his dogs so the offer was declined.

Later, when the two princesses were told about what had happened, Countess Granville was informed that they would have liked to have received the cat. This stimulated speculation that it would be forwarded to the Palace after all. However, it never was. Perhaps everyone remembered the king's verdict about the dogs.

* The Queen Mother eventually became the owner of a Manx cat - but not in her personal capacity.

For a time it became ship's cat aboard the royal yacht Britannia.

The three month old brown tabby, Manninagh Schickrys, along with an illuminated pedigree, was presented to Her Majesty by Castletown Commissioners when she visited the town in August 1963.

Schickrys spent eleven years in royal service, his declining years when he suffered from a kidney tumour, at the Portsmouth home of Britannia's chief petty officer Ian Denny. Eventually Schickrys had to be 'put to sleep' in July 1974 - co-incidentally on July 5th, the Island's traditional national day.

Laugh and Grow Fat.

Kys ta Shiu?

The overhand stroke is a capital joke,
But a tail would play "Old Harry"—
And might lead to a "bite,"
Which (apart from the fright)
Is an extra weight to carry.

My name's Tommy Kelly, I own,
An' I live at the back of Marown
My father's no fule, he was born
      at Barrule,
My mother's birthplace, Ballabroole,
I've sisters and cousins by the score
      and half dozens
At Crossag, Poolvash, Balladoole,

I've an aunt out at Colby, another at Sulby,
More at Ballasalla, Ballough, Ballahonny,
Ballaglass, Balacraine, Ballacowle, Gobyvolley,
Ballakelley, Ballagawne, Ballacratch, Ballacrink,
And a good many more if I'd more time to think,

I've a sweetheart out there at
      Glenmooar,
I might have had one or two
      more,
There was one at Baregarrow,
      and then Cronkymarrow,
And a little dark cat at Ballure,
Two at Cronkyoodie, sweet Tilly
      and Susie,
Knocksharry Knockchuckeley,
Knock y yorry, Glen Crutchery,
Attentions polite there near led
      to butchery,
If there's more I'm not very sure.

Walt Disney and "Manxie"

When Mickey Mouse became the cartoon star of cinemas throughout the world, imaginative minds in the Isle of Man wondered: What was the use of a mouse without a cat?

And if Mickey ever had a tailless "friend" what publicity that would be for the Isle of Man!

So it was that a plan was devised for a young Walt Disney to receive the gift of a Manx cat.

Perhaps that might inspire him, it was thought, to include a rumpy among his future cartoon characters.

The idea of a Manx cat reaching film stardom had concentrated minds on the Isle of Man eversince the black-bodied and white-faced Felix had been

Felix the film cat turns Manx at Douglas

popularised in cartoons by Pathe.

For one story most of his tail had been cut off, making him a stumpy. So popular was this on the Isle of Man that simple pot vases for sale to tourists were marketed in the 1920s with black transfer prints on them depicting Felix minus most of his tail. "Felix the Film Cat Turns Manx at Douglas," said the caption.

It *was* a collaboration between the Publicity Board at Douglas and the editor/proprietor of the Isle of Man Examiner and Member of the House of Keys, T.R. Radcliffe, that led to Disney getting his cat in the summer of 1933.

The North American Manx Association was planning a Convention later that year in Chicago. To satisfy demand among Manx expatriates there for Manx cats, local breeder George Cave was raising some kittens for export to Chicago in time for the Convention. That inspired "T.R." to suggest to the Publicity Board: Why not send Walt Disney a Manx cat as a gift at the same time? It might inspire the creation of a cartoon character.

So it was arranged through Disney's London agent. Officially the giver was the Island's Lt-Governor. Walt Disney, meanwhile, agreed to accept the gift.

That June a fourteen month old jet black Manx cat from a farm at Braddan, described as "a splendid specimen of his race" and named Manxie was taken to Liverpool by Mr Radcliffe on the first leg of his journey to Hollywood and possible fame. Arriving at Liverpool at mid-day one Saturday aboard the Steam Packet

Company's vessel, the ss Manxman, Manxie was taken immediately to the Cunard liner Franconia which was due to sail to New York within the hour and given into the charge of the liner's butcher: an appropriate chaperon, it was thought, considering his access to the meat supplies.

With him Manxie brought feeding instructions: He liked to be fed twice a day, at 8am and four in the afternoon

"Manxie" Leaves For Hollywood
FINE SEND OFF FROM LIVERPOOL
WHAT HE TOLD THE PRESS :
If "Manxie", the pure-bred Manx cat, which is now on its way to Hollywood to

and had a good, healthy appetite. He wasn't "faddy" but had been reared on boiled milk, raw meat and fish without stint.

Awaiting Manxie to give him a well orchestrated send-off was a battery of press photographers.

How did the Manx cat lose its tail? they wanted to know.

No idea, said "T.R." He supposed it would remain a mystery. All he could say on behalf of Manxie was that the prospect of meeting Mickey Mouse tickled Manxie to death.

After an uneventful Atlantic crossing Manxie was accepted in New York on behalf of Walt Disney by representatives of the United Artists Corporation.

Manxie was guest of honour at a reception then sent by train to

Hollywood - "heavily insured," it was claimed, because of his pedigreed lineage.

His arrival was announced in the Los Angeles Times with the suggestion: Mickey Mouse had a new playmate.

Walt Disney promptly cabled the Lt-Governor in the Isle of Man: "Cat arrived OK. A million thanks. Where's the tail?"

Manxie became a popular resident of the Disney studio in the years leading up to the production of the classic "Snow White and the Seven Dwarfs."

But it wasn't as Manxie that everyone came to know him. Walt gave him the new name of "W.E.C." - short for "World Economic Conference." Like the cat's tail, he predicted, in these dark days of Economic Depression and mass unemployment, he expected the conference to be cut short!

Two years later in June 1935 whilst in London at the beginning of a European tour Walt Disney contemplated a visit to what he called "the land of the tailless cat," but couldn't make it. In a letter to the secretary of the Isle of Man's Publicity Board, however, he reported: W.E.C. had become "a real pet with everyone in the studio." Unfortunately the cat had developed a fondness for automobile riding. On seeing a stationery car he would jump into it regardless of the fact that when the car started he might be taken many miles away. This had happened on several occasions and in one case the studio had had to pay $25 to get him back.

"Everybody makes a great fuss of him and he certainly seems to enjoy life," wrote Mr Disney, "although if he continues to indulge in stolen car rides there is no knowing what will happen to him."

What did remains a mystery. Today there is no record in the Walt Disney archives that Manxie or W.E.C. ever existed. Mr Radcliffe's daughter remembers, however, reading in a Forces newspaper during the Second World War that Mr Disney was asked during a visit to Cairo: How many pets did he have? and he replied: Only one; a Manx cat.

Thereafter no more was heard of Manxie. His likeness didn't appear even in "The Aristocats," that Disney feature-length classic about cats.

For some reason the concept of a tailless cat didn't appeal to the Disney animators...though it did to others.

Significantly in the same year as Walt Disney considered visiting the Isle of Man it was announced on the Island that production was expected to start soon in Britain on a sound cartoon series featuring a Manx cat.

Frank Tipper Jnr, formerly of the Walt Disney studio and the Warner Bros unit responsible for Silly Symphonies, was reported to have left America for negotiations in London on a series to be known as "Manx Kitty."

Had that been inspired by Manxie? It's tempting to suppose that it had.

Sadly nothing further was heard of the idea.

Walt Disney's Manx cat may have disappeared, re-named and unaccounted for long ago but Manxie lives on...in story books.

He's a different Manxie, generations apart, but he's all black, like the original...the creation of Isle of Man housewife and accounts clerk Pam Way of 39 Douglas Street, Peel.

One day a stray long-tailed brindle cat came calling. Pam called her Kit. Then Kit brought another surprise: a litter in which there were two kittens which Pam knew she must keep also: a marmalade stumpy with so many stripes he reminded her of American T.V.'s comic Sergeant Bilko so she called him Bilko and another, pure rumpy, all black, which she called Manxie.

It was appropriate, she thought, for she had just started writing and publishing illustrated children's books about an imaginary black rumpy named Manxie.

First, in 1982, there had been "Introducing Manxie," followed later that year by "Manxie Goes Sailing." Then had come "Manxie Goes to London." Eventually there were more books: "Manxie Gets Married," "Manxie Down Under" (in Australia) and "Manxie Goes West." All described how the absence of a tail somehow saved Manxie's life.

Tragically, however, whilst in fiction Manxie had nine lives like most cats the real Manxie had just one and lost it whilst only four in an accident.

Later, Pam's seven year old grandson told friends at school: There'd be no more Manxie books because Manxie had died.

The spirit of Manxie lives on, however - on television. Walt Disney's pet may never have made it to the big screen but Pam's made it to television. In 1992 after the BBC had heard of the Manxie books, the pre-school "Playdays" programme for children introduced a series of illustrated stories. These started to be broadcast in October that year and since then have been syndicated to television stations elsewhere in the world.

Kys ta Shiu?

SWISS COTTAGE. GLEN HELEN

Ellan Vannin veg veén.

Kys ta Shiu?

We are the cats that   come from manx land,
We tell no "tales" for   we have no "tails" to tell.

"Just a line" is what
we say—
When out on the tiles
till the break of day,
'Tis the only tail we
can manage to find—
You've had it "before"
(as we've none
behind.)

Kys ta Shiu ?

Ellan Vannin. veg veen.

H. M. S. *Manxman*

At least six Manx cats have been Royal Navy mascots since 1940 - five of them aboard the minesweeper HMS Manxman, reputed at one time to be the fastest vessel in the navy.

One of them even caused a minor "international incident!"

The first rumpy was presented to the Manxman when the vessel was commissioned in Battle of Britain year, 1940. Sadly the cat was lost at sea during the war so in December 1946 when the Manxman paid an official visit to Douglas, the Commander, Captain George Oswald, was given a replacement along with a water colour painting and 300 year old map of the Island for the wardroom.

In time this puss was lost too but as the Manxman was "mothballed" no immediate replacement was appropriate. In September 1951, however, she was recommissioned. Prior to her embarking on a two year tour of duty in the Mediterranean she paid another courtesy visit to Douglas and the Mayor, Councillor Tom Radcliffe, presented her Commander, Captain Trevor Lean DSO, with a third Manx rumpy, a fine ginger specimen called Orry. Supposedly it was a tom - hence the name, that of a revered Manx Viking king. Only later was it established that she was female.

Orry was reported by the captain shortly afterwards as having settled in. She was "thoroughly at home," he wrote. However, she was nearly lost in a dramatic incident at Port Said.

When the Manxman tied up alongside the cruiser Liverpool the latter's cat decided on an unauthorised inspection tour. A startled Orry fled straight overboard into the sea and was saved only by the prompt action of Scottish officer, Lt Lawson. He stripped off his uniform and dived into the sea after her.

It *was* in October 1952 that the "international incident" occurred.

Whilst Manxman was visiting Naples, Orry went A.W.O.L. She couldn't be found which wasn't really surprising as she must have had a strong instinct to explore ashore. Her home town of Douglas, after all, was sometimes called the Naples of the North. Eventually the Manxman had to leave port without her. A request was left with the authorities in Naples to look out for her.

Subsequently Orry was found by a woman in a castle overlooking Naples and caused a furore in the Italian press. Was this an example of what British sailors did to their cats? they demanded. They cut off their tails?

To calm everyone the British Consulate had to issue a detailed explanation about Orry's origins.

Orry, meanwhile, was delivered to the British Consulate, flown to Malta then passed to a liaison officer at NATO headquarters, Southern Europe who arranged for her to be returned to the Manxman.

By then she was heavily pregnant and soon afterwards delivered three kittens, one of them a stumpy with just the vestige of a tail.

In a telegram to the Mayor of Douglas, Manxman's captain confessed: "Father's nationality uncertain."

The Mayor replied: "Suggest Manxman visits the Isle of Man to obtain mate for Orry. May prevent international incident and future uncertainty in the nationality of offspring."

Sadly Orry died in March 1953 after contracting an infection whilst Manxman was visiting Gibraltar. Her stumpy offspring, appropriately named Stumpy and described as having a coat that was "a camouflage mixture" of tabby and ginger, was adopted as the ship's new mascot.

Captain R. E. Washbourn who wrote to the Island with the news, said: "We were all very saddened by the tragedy when it overtook us. Orry and her family were very much a part of the ship's company and we were very fond of them."

Eventually Stumpy was lost too.

The cat tradition continued when a new 3,000 ton Royal Navy forward support ship for minesweepers named H.M.S. Manxman was commissioned at Chatham in February 1963. On behalf of the Isle of Man's Government, the Island's chief judge, Deemster Sydney Kneale (who represented the Lt-Governor) presented the ship's captain, Lt-Cmdr A. L. Cawston, with Kelly, a Manx kitten.

Later, when the ship sailed for the Far East the navy had an equally appropriate appointment as official cat-minder. Who better than a Manxman too?

Kelly was placed in the care of ship's postman and senior quartermaster, 37-year-old Leading Seaman William Charmer whose wife and family lived at 14 Church Street, Peel. Later he said Kelly could be found asleep either in the wardroom mess or on a pile of newspapers on one of the ratings' messdecks.

Only one thing blighted Kelly's life on the ocean wave. That was George the ship's dog, acquired by the crew in Hong Kong. So strained did relations become that the two were discouraged from mingling.

• HMS Barrosa, a battle class destroyer, received a ten week old rumpy in July 1957.

Named Manxman, the kitten was given to the destroyer's crew by Mayor of Douglas, Councillor Bill Kaneen, when the vessel was visiting the town.

• Another vessel named Manxman - this time one of the Steam Packet Company's fleet - acquired a Manx cat when the ferry was sold to English businessmen. They wanted a Manx cat to maintain the Manxness of the vessel.

A nine month old stray black and white female Manx, found at Orrisdale in the spring of 1983, was flown to Blackpool and then taken by white Rolls Royce to Preston Docks where the Manxman was berthed.

At first there were fears that she might not get on well with the ship's resident parrot, Horatio, but it was reported later: They became the best of pals.

Good-bye to the Isle of Man.

| Douglas 24 . VIII . 1909

Cat among the pigeons at Whitehall!

It had all the hallmarks of an international incident... Fighting in the gardens of 10 Downing Street! On the right a Siamese; on the left, a Manxie.

Worse, when the wife of prime minister Harold Wilson, rushed to intervene on her pet Siamese's behalf, she ended up with scratches.

Such scandalous goings-on in Whitehall! tut-tutted senior civil servants and pointed the finger of blame straight at the Home Office. There lay the culprit, they were sure.

Name: Peta. Occupation: Official mouser. Pay: Five shillings (25p) a year. The charge: lambasting the nation's top cat!

Horrified Home Office staff protested: The accusation was false. It must have been some other cat. But really the circumstantial evidence was enough.

How many black tailless cats were there roaming the corridors of power at Whitehall? Thus did Peta end up in the "dog house."

Peta was the gift of the Isle of Man to the Home Office in 1964: the last official mouser, elevated to the exhalted position of having a properly-designated Civil Service allowance. She was a feline women's libber too for traditionally the post had been occupied by a tom!

Hence her name of Peta: a reminder that previous incumbents of her post had been male and known as Peter.

The unique cat tradition began in 1883 when the Home Office, then occupying mouse-infested offices, was granted official permission to "employ" an official mouser. Generations of cats thereafter became a popular sight, sat before office fires whilst the business of the nation was conducted within their hearing. A particularly popular resting place was a stone plinth at the foot of the stairs in the entrance hall. Nearby was a showcase containing trophies won by the Home Office Sports Association so in time, imagining that the cats were mounting guard over the trophies, members adopted the official mouser as their mascot.

The initial allowance for the cat was one old penny a day; enough to keep it well fed and watered. Extra costs for emergencies had to be approved by the Deputy Finance Officer. Hence the minute he recorded in the 1940s when one particular cat was run over by a car and had to be put to sleep by the R. S. P. C. A.:

"I note that a coup d'etat
Deprived us of the office cat.
Two bob well spent, without a doubt,
To help poor Peter peter out."

It was following another death that Peta arrived on the scene: the first true pedigree puss to be recruited by the Home Office. Her starting allowance was an unprecedented double that of her predecessor - perhaps because of her "underground" contacts, suggested one newspaper.

MANNINAGH KATEDHU

Presented by the Isle of Man Government to the Home Office in May, 1964, and renamed "Peta." She was a permanent member of the staff and received a weekly wage of 5/- as "official mouser."

Lt-Governor in the Isle of Man, Sir Ronald Garvey (ever alive to an opportunity to publicise the Island), arranged with the local Board of Agriculture to supply an appropriate kitten from its Cattery and Peta was the result. Officially her pedigree name was Manninagh KateDhu but the Home Office decided: Peta would be her pet name to keep the old tradition alive.

Secretary to the Board of Agriculture, Wilf Halsall, and Board veterinary officer, Douglas Kerruish, took her to London that May and the Home Secretary accepted her: a time-consuming business as fog delayed the departure of the Manx party by a day and so screwed up prior arrangements.

One irritated civil servant was heard to moan: "A whole day's been wasted over this blessed cat." Later a local newspaper observed: "What a fuss over a puss." But Sir Ronald Garvey's intention of achieving national publicity for the Island was achieved.

Accompanying Peta was an illuminated pedigree prepared by Manx artist John Nicholson.

Prophetically it included between the names of her sire and dam the drawing of a flying pigeon - implying she would "put the cat among the pigeons" at Whitehall.

And so she did with the fight at Number 10!

More irritating, however, for senior civil servants was her noisy miaowing around the building and lapses in toilet training.

Finally, when Peta was featured on the cover of a Home Office Christmas card important questions were asked:

Was it right that a Government department responsible for legislation concerning cruelty to animals should keep a pedigree cat "in conditions that might be held to be less than ideal?"

That concentrated minds and eventually it was suggested that a "pussy's paradise" - namely, a patch of grass which could be used exclusively by Peta - should be laid out in the inner quadrangle at the Home Office building.

So it might have been too - but for the fact that the Home Office was to be transferred to new rodent-free offices at Queen Anne's Gate. Then there would be no need for a puss at all, it was reckoned.

Thus a tradition ended. In the parlance of the Home Office, Peta was given the "golden paw-shake" and eased into early retirement, boarding out with a Civil Servant who had befriended her until her death at the age of 16 in early 1980.

HOME OFFICE

HOME OFFICE

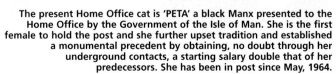

The present Home Office cat is 'PETA' a black Manx presented to the
Home Office by the Government of the Isle of Man. She is the first
female to hold the post and she further upset tradition and established
a monumental precedent by obtaining, no doubt through her
underground contacts, a starting salary double that of her
predecessors. She has been in post since May, 1964.

(From official Home Office Christmas card.)

How Scotland won – the "Tail" of the Manx kitten

The cartoon says it all . . .A Manx cat at the centre of the soccer world's needle match of the year in 1927 - the international at Hampden Park between England and Scotland!

He was the team's official mascot, giving the cartoonist at the Glasgow Daily Record ample scope to speculate on how he might have helped the team if permitted on the pitch.

As a publicity stunt it was probably the Island's biggest coup with a rumpy: aimed at publicising the Island among potential Scottish holidaymakers.

Newspapers were full of it. There was a full page advertisement extolling the Island in the official programme and 50,000 booklets about the Island and plans for a Scottish week that summer including a Highland Games were distributed throughout Glasgow.

It was all the brain-child of editor/proprietor of the Isle of Man Examiner, "T.R." Radcliffe.

Through the Examiner and its Saturday sports paper, the Green Final, a special trip to see the match was organised for Isle of Man soccer enthusiasts. A ferry to the Scottish port of Ardrossan was chartered for them, a special train laid on to take them to Glasgow and once there charabancs took them on scenic tours prior to the match.

Upwards of 800 rosetted and flag-waving enthusiasts from the Island descended on Glasgow in a fleet of charabancs - a propaganda mission which Mr Radcliffe believed was the biggest of its kind ever undertaken by the Island. Giant flags borrowed from Isle of Man Steam Packet vessels flew from vehicle bonnets, hopefully reminding those who saw them of past holidays in the Isle of Man.

Mr Radcliffe's travelling companion was an all black Manx kitten obtained from local breeder George Cave.

At a gathering of members of Scotland's team in the dressing room prior to the big match he presented the rumpy to skipper Jimmy McMullan. There were a few scratches, a rueful Mr Radcliffe was to recall later, but nothing too severe. Among others eager to hold the new mascot was outside left Alan Morton, about to play his 22nd international for Scotland.

The cat was then taken into the grandstand to "watch" the match and afterwards Jimmy McMullan took him home with him to Manchester where his wife kept puss as a family pet.

Manx publicity, meanwhile, came to a climax with all the Manx fans gathering in Glasgow's densely packed Central Station and singing the Manx song "Ellan Vannin."

Manx cats in Music and Song

The Manx cat has inspired few songs. One, however, captivated America's University of Harvard. It became the Song of Harvard in 1915. "The Cats" or "Feline Fantasy" was unearthed by William Bradley Breed for the university's tenth reunion in 1915 and was played in Symphony Hall by the Boston Pops Orchestra, conducted by him.

Curiously it was a Harvard-based man who many years later, in the 1980s, dismissed Manx cats as not being a separate breed at all.

After extensive research into the tailless phenomenon Neil B. Todd of the Animal Research Centre at Harvard Medical School said Manxies belonged to one of eight shorthaired breeds already recognised in the U.S.A. "Manx cats are best thought of as cats afflicted with a syndrome which happens to have a genetic base," he said.

In 1928 Francis Day and Horton published "Would a Manx Cat wag its tail (if it had one)?" - the composer, Julian Wright and lyricist, William E. Haines. The song sheet was adorned by a picture of a Manx cat.

The verdict in the Isle of Man?

"The words are silly," said the *Examiner*.

In 1950 L. A. Bancroft composed

Attractions of Mona—An Invitation.

Reg. 54. E.M. No. A6. Copyright No. 58,306. All rights reserved.

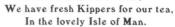

We have the Dog with three legs,
With three legs, with three legs,
We have the Dog with three legs,
In the lovely Isle of Man.

We have the Cat without the tail,
Without the tail, without the tail,
We have the Cat without the tail,
In the lovely Isle of Man.

We have the Hens without the tails,
Without the tails, without the tails,
We have the hens without the tails,
In the lovely Isle of Man.

We have fresh Kippers for our tea,
For our tea, for our tea,
We have fresh Kippers for our tea,
In the lovely Isle of Man.

We have the fairest of all Maids,
Of all Maids, of all Maids,
We have the fairest of all Maids,
In the lovely Isle of Man.

CHORUS, *after each verse.*
So, come and have a Jolly Time,
Jolly Time, Jolly Time,
So, come and have a Jolly Time,
In the lovely Isle of Man.

Song of Harvard 1915

the promotional song "Go Abroad to the Isle of Man." With the rise of the Mediterranean resorts it was intended to highlight the Island's differences to the U.K., featuring on the song sheet cover a palm tree, the sea and a rumpy. The words included the line "You'll even see the cats out there without any tails."

* Only one official recording is known to exist of a Manx cat's miaow. It's in stereo and included in a cassette "The Wonderful World of Mann," produced by international bandleader and composer Ronnie Aldrich as a gesture of appreciation for his life in the Isle of Man. The cassette features many atmospheric

sounds of Manx life.

The miaows come from three pure black Manxies acquired by Ronnie and his wife Mary from a litter of four at the Howe. One was called Mona, another Kelly and the third Nelson (despite being a girl) because one eye was late to open.

Kys to Shiu?

SUGAR LOAF ROCK.

SONG OF THE MANX CAT.

A tale of the night, and a tale of the day,
A tale of the cat who has gone astray,
Tales of sorrow, and tales of glee,
Most things have tales,
But theres no tail on me.

COPYRIGHT.

Ellan Vannin

QUOCUNQUE JECERIS STABIT

A Rumpy Club!

Meet Rumpy. He's a cartoon character modelled on the Manx cat. Members of the Isle of Man team which competed in the Commonwealth Games in Edmonton, Canada in 1978 carried badges of him and many were swapped for mementoes of the Games from other competitors.

Rumpy was a cartoon mascot who helped fund the Manx team's expenses.

Hopes of making him an international star, however, never materialised.

The whole thing started one day in 1975 when a group of Manx and English businessmen including Manx sportsman Brian Whitehead (a director of Business and Leisure Promotions Ltd which was involved in leisure activities in Blackpool) met there to discuss ways of raising money for a Manx team to be entered in the Commonwealth Games. What the team needed, they decided, was a mascot which could be used by commercial concerns on a royalty basis.

The Wombles of Wimbledon Common had been a commercial success. So too Paddington Bear. If a new character like them could be devised they reckoned they could be on to a winner.

The Manx cat seemed the logical choice; the name Rumpy, appealing. A cartoonist doodled and produced a character around which everything else would be based. The character was registered throughout the world

to protect it and a new company, Rumpy Ltd, was formed with a commitment that a percentage of all turnover would go to charity - the first £20,000 to the Commonwealth Games team.

A Rumpy song was planned and negotiations commenced with a television company for the production of a cartoon series featuring Rumpy and other proposed Manx cat friends. These would be the vehicles, it was envisaged, by which the Rumpy character could be publicised throughout the world. Then they could be exploited commercially.

By early 1976 a Rumpy Club for youngsters had been formed through which it was hoped Rumpy branded goods could be marketed by mail order. The ambitious plan was for club branches to be formed not only in Britain but in America and Canada too. Members would get a wallet,

identity card, club badge and a news bulletin containing news, stories, competitions and a mail order section.

One of the first products to be produced was a Rumpy soft toy but other items were proposed - like a Rumpy jigsaw, a hand puppet, 3-D posters, watches and clocks. A Blackpool firm showed interest also in the production of cream and jam biscuits in the shape of Rumpy. This didn't materialise in the end but Rumpy wrappers for ice cream produced by Manx Ices did.

A small shop in Peel Road, Douglas was opened to help promote sales on the Island. Elsewhere it was planned to enrol salespeople.

For the summer of 1976 a Rumpy outfit with a giant cat's head was made for someone to wear at Island events like the agricultural shows. A Rumpy competition involving a treasure hunt for summer visitors was organised too, people buying a questionaire for 25p. On this were 40 simple questions about the Island. On submitting their answers they had to enclose specified items found on the Island such as an M.E.R. ticket or a film wrapper.

Whatever happened to Rumpy thereafter?

Sadly like so many other bright ideas, he just faded away. Lyrics were written for his song but the music was never composed.

Said Brian Whitehead: "Once money had been raised for the Commonwealth Games the people involved just went their different ways."

Feathered rumpies too!

Taillessness is not exclusive to cats. There is a form of rumpy bantam too, publicised well in the late Victorian and Edwardian era as the "Manx rooster." Souvenir china and printed material included it along with the Manx cat and the mythical three-legged Manxman. It's a small game bird, now rare, the male weighing usually no more than 26 ounces, the hen usually about four ounces less.

Officially its origins are given as "Great Britain" but a book on British poultry standards says that it is "not uncommon in the Isle of Man."

It has been claimed that the rumpy originated from South America and that Victorian breeders in the Isle of Man, proud of the Island's association with taillessness because of the Manx cat, merely "adopted" the bird as being Manx too. However, oral tradition among successive local breeders disputes this. The South American bird lays blue eggs, the Manx rumpy, tinted white ones, they say, so there must be a difference.

Their claim is that the bird is a mutation of the English Game Bantam just as the Manx cat is a mutation of the British Shorthair cat.

As is the case with Manx cats they don't always breed true. Occasionally a longtailed bantam can be born. Billy McCoubrie, an Isle of Man Steam Packet company quayside checker of Little Mill, Onchan who breeds them and other game birds as a hobby, believes it may be because of a practice by veteran breeders to use tailed birds in their breeding programmes occasionally to strengthen future chicks.

Alan Preston of Port Erin, harbour keeper at Port St Mary, who has five males and ten females in his breeding stock, agrees. "Breed rumpy to rumpy for too long, you will usually find that they will die out," he says. "You have to introduce a long tail from time to time."

Geo. B. Cowen, Art Photographer, Ramsey, I.O.M.

Natives.

In 1836 architect John Welch, who was responsible for the designing of the Tower of Refuge in Douglas Bay, referred to the fowls in a short guide book "A Six Days Tour in the Isle of Man by a Stranger." They were called rumpies, he said. As they inter-bred, however, with the more favoured English breeds on the Island some had a quarter of a tail, half a tail, three quarters of a tail and a full tail "according to some scale of deserts with which I am unacquainted."

In the 1880s the Rev Theophilus Talbot recorded that there were numerous fowls on the Isle of Man without tail feathers. He had it on good authority that there was a tailless duck too.

Taillessness in other species wasn't a curiousity confined to the Isle of Man, however, he said. In 1743 tailless fowl had been recorded in France and a guide to the Isle of Islay, referring to Kildalton on the east of the island claimed: "Among the natural curiousities of this district is a fresh water loch, the trout in which have no tails."

Today there are only a handful of Manx breeders but once there were a great many. Public awareness of the birds was much greater, too, because of their appearance at annual Fur and Feather shows. Their exhibition at local shows has been traced to the 1890s by Alan Preston.

In 1925 the Scottish island of Arran claimed the tailless fowl as its own, that it was indigenous to that island, but Isle of Man breeders retaliated with counter-claims that it was known as the Manx Rumpy and as such had appeared at local poultry shows for years.

Among Manx breeders responsible for perpetuating the variety in the latter part of the 20th century were the late "Tonty" Wylde of Lezayre and Eric Hall of The Braaid. In the 1970s when the breeding of rumpies was going out of fashion elsewhere Eric Hall was largely responsible for keeping the variety alive. Thus, when interest in them revived, he was able to supply birds to other breeders.

It was from Eric Hall that Alan Preston got his birds.

In Mona's Isle, once. long ago,
A cat ; whilst in a yard did spy
A chicken walking to and fro ,
At which she cast a wicked eye.

Puss ran and caught it by the tail !
Deprived of which the chicken flew.
Chased by a dog, poor pussy frail,
In turn had her tail bit off too.

All cats and fowls in Manxland seen,
E'er after that, have tailless been.

L. Bros. & Co., Stratford, E,

Series S.

The Manx Cattery

For more than twenty years the accepted cradle of the Manx cat was an official breeding cattery in the Isle of Man: launched by the Manx Government, administered and funded later by Douglas Corporation. From here originated many of the world's top pedigree stock: the founders of dynasties of champions all over the world.

They were pampered and doted upon.

When pregnant females were about to give birth there was someone usually there to hold a paw, stroke a belly and give reassurance.

Mrs Sheila Quaggin, now an independent breeder of Woodbourne Road, Douglas, used to be one of those responsible for them with Sylvia Potts.

"It was my life, seven days a week, sometimes until eleven at night," she said. "At Christmas I remember we used to prepare turkey for them and there would be presents for them, all in wrapping paper. People who had visited the place and fallen in love with a certain cat used to send Christmas cards from their own cats, sometimes with pictures of them and we would hang them up."

Her most enduring memory was the arrival one day in a school party of a blind and handicapped young girl. She was given a kitten to cuddle and began squealing. At first Mrs Quaggin thought the girl was afraid. Then she realised: No. The girl wasn't distressed. She was squealing with delight and excitement.

"That will stay with me forever," said Mrs Quaggin.

Today the Manx Cattery doesn't exist. Responsibility for the perpetuation of the tailless cat on the Isle of Man is left partly to nature with its random births of rumpies and stumpies and partly to small breeding catteries run by private individuals.

Some provide pedigrees. Others don't.

A few exchange kittens to introduce new blood into their breeding stocks to prevent inbreeding but some confess they don't know who the other breeders are.

Once there was a club to liaise between them but apathy led to its closure and suggested revivals have never stirred enough interest.

Thus the situation is very much as it was in the 19th century. Nature takes its course - with human intervention just helping it along.

The story of the cattery has its origins in what happened in May 1932. That was when it was claimed there were too many cats in the Isle of Man.

During a debate in the House of Keys on new legislation to protect wild birds, Christopher Shimmin suggested: forget about the threat humans were to birds, think instead about the damage cats did. Many birds didn't get a chance to get to old

Cattery photographs courtesy
Sheila Quaggin

age. To protect birds the government should limit the number of cats on the Island by introducing licences for them.

The idea went mostly ignored. It was notable only for what happened the following week.

Curiously the Chicago Tribune reported the "alarming news" that Manx cats were threatened by extinction.

Was that possible? In an Island where an M.H.K. had said there were too many cats, clearly mostly of the long-tailed variety, had the gene-pool that produced rumpies in litters suddenly dried up?

Not so. There were plenty of cats. The problem was that rumpies were in such demand elsewhere in the world and among visiting tourists that they were being exported. The Tribune said the result was that the tailless cat was disappearing from the streets and from that drew the conclusion that the rumpy within the Isle of Man was threatened by extinction.

What was overlooked was the fact that the gene for taillessness remained among many of the Island's tailed cats so a new generation of rumpies could emerge later.

Two years later a regular topical column in the Mona's Herald entitled "At the Sign of the Manx Cat" and ostensibly written by one sounded a further warning. It was written tongue in cheek but there was a serious aspect to it.

Some weeks earlier in a report of the Onchan Fur and Feather Show the Mona's Herald had reported: "A few years ago Manx cats were merely tolerated as a curiosity but fanciers today appear to be treating the breed with the greatest respect."

Now the feline column warned: "Something has got to be done about this Manx cat business and done quickly if another of our fine industries is not to languish and eventually expire."

There had been reports that Japan had sent secret emissaries to the Island to procure a selection of cats so that Japan could capture the world market in them. "With oriental methods of mass production and low wages," said the column, "we cannot hope to compete with wholesale dumping in the markets of the world."

The Island needed to organise and protect its "industry," said the column. English newspapers had suggested that a tax should be levied on the importation into the Island of non-Manx cats to protect the breed. Certainly the Island's Board of Agriculture needed a broader vision of the future. The importation of tailed

Greeba as a two-year old. Born 1 . IV . 88

cats needed to be restricted to a licensing system operated by a Manx Cat Producers Association. A subsidy should be given in respect of each litter bred and the homes of people engaged in the production of Manx cats should be exempted from local authority rates.

Clearly the suggestions were a parody on the problems of international trade. They weren't intended to be taken seriously nor were they. However, there was an element of sense in them.

Fourteen years and one world war later, after another cycle of good births of rumpies and exports, a Denver newspaper in the U.S.A. reported in the autumn of 1949 that to ensure the survival of the Manx cat the Isle of Man had decided to ban exports and imports of tailed cats would be prohibited too.

It was wrong. But the story had a basis in fact.

Basil Megaw, Director of the Manx Museum, was concerned about new reports of increased exports. If all locally-born rumpies were exported, he wondered, could the Manx cat variety eventually become extinct?

This concern was heightened after the visit to the Island in December 1950 to act as a judge at a fur and feather show of Mr J. Caseby of Southport. He urged the Island to form a Manx Cat Society which could govern the registration of local Manx cat pedigrees. Hardly anyone concerned themselves with such records. The birth of Manx cats was considered just a natural everyday occurrence.

Initial reaction to Mr Caseby's suggestion was muted. Most Manx people were interested in cats only as pets, not show animals. However, his observations helped prompt deliberation about the future of the variety.

Finally in 1952, in search of an answer to the fears over exports, Mr Megaw wrote to Liverpool University where Ruth Bisbee had conducted research into Manx cats some years earlier with a colleague, Dr Herdman.

At first he was reassured. The probability was that only rumpies were exported, she said. Stumpies wouldn't be wanted yet they carried the gene for taillessness so should be capable of keeping the Manx cat variety going on the Island indefinitely.

In theory she was correct but she overlooked a vital point which John Colman of the university's Marine Biological Station at Port Erin was quick to seize upon.

Stumpies ought to function as a "reserve," he said, but they weren't surviving to do so. The practice on the Island was for stumpies to be included among the unwanted kittens in litters. Usually they were drowned at birth.

Thereafter, local people were encouraged to keep stumpies rather than destroy them and so began the first moves to preserve the variety.

The next move happened in January 1953. At a meeting in Parkfield,

MANX CAT

Douglas an Isle of Man Manx Cat Association was formed. Its intention: "to encourage, preserve and improve the breeding of Manx cats."

One of its first pieces of advice after a study of accidental and controlled matings was: Mate two good rumpies together and the progeny were often poor.

Chairman of the Association was Government Vet Douglas Kerruish; its secretary, Manx cat breeder Jessie Twining of Kerro-ny-Clough Cottage, Greeba. Mr Kerruish had practised as a private vet on the Island since 1932 then four years later had become the Island's first Government Vet. As such he had been to the forefront in the eradication of T.B. in Manx cattle and other diseases ahead of the rest of Britain. His interest in Manx cats had resulted in him lecturing on the subject and being a judge at shows both on and off the Island.

From cover of
"Manx Journal of Agriculture".

Former Executive Council chairman and later president of Tynwald, Sir Charles Kerruish, creditted Mr Kerruish with the inspiration for the establishment of a Manx Government Cattery. Yet curiously in 1954 Mr Kerruish was confident that there was no threat to the cats. He believed numbers to be increasing - perhaps because of greater public interest stimulated by publicity.

It took seven years, a cat 'flu epidemic and more exports for him to think differently. Unofficial estimates put the Island's population of Manx cats then at about 350; maybe not enough to sustain the variety indefinitely. Mr Kerruish argued that a nucleus of breeding stock should be preserved.

Thus was conceived the idea of a Government Cattery.

Peel M.H.K., George Gale, a member of the Board of Agriculture, persuaded the Board in early March to establish a cattery at the government's experimental farm of Knockaloe near Peel.

Purchased by the Manx Government in 1923 with funds from the estate of one of the Island's greatest benefactors, Henry Bloom Noble, Knockaloe was primarily an experimental breeding station for livestock and a centre for the production of pedigree strains of oat, barley, wheat and potatoes but there was nowhere else as appropriate for the breeding of cats within government control at the time so the responsibility was allocated to the farm.

Overseeing it was Agricultural Organiser, Scotsman George Howie. He had made Knockaloe and the development of Manx agriculture his life's work ever since coming to the Island in 1927. Now he was confronted by one of the more curious aspects of his job. When he retired he planned to write a book about Manx agriculture and for that purpose had accumulated notes on the backs of outdated official documents. The cattery would have featured in it. But tragically he died before he could proceed further and his notes were lost in a bonfire of what were presumed to be unimportant papers. Thus was lost what could have been a fascinating insight into the cattery's early days.

The venture was a low-profile project, undertaken with the minimum of fuss and publicity.

The Isle of Man Times of November 3rd, 1961 devoted just one paragraph to it: "Manx cats at Knockaloe? Yes, it's true. There is a special section for breeding rumpies - and a jolly good idea too!"

Five days later it was confirmed at a meeting of the Board of Agriculture and minuted that sufficient progress had been made in the creation of accommodation for cats at Knockaloe that cats could now be placed there and in the next few weeks they were: by the beginning of December, a total of seven including one which was considered to be a particularly fine specimen.

Immediately it received international publicity there were requests for kittens from as far apart as the U.S.A. and Ethiopia but all enquirers received the same reply: There would be none available for sale as yet. They would be kept to build up a "breeding nucleus." Only when there was a surplus above requirements would any be sold.

That exports would be considered eventually was a surprise given that the nature of the cattery was to ensure the survival of the cats within the Isle of Man. However, the level of world interest which promised to promote knowledge of the Isle of Man as a low tax area presumably persuaded government officials into accepting the very export policy which had helped lead to the need for the cattery in the first place. Local interest in expensive pedigree cats, meanwhile, was minimal. Most people were too accustomed to getting their rumpy pets either free or for only a small charge from friends and neighbours.

The first person in charge of the cattery was Mrs May Teare, later of 13 North View, Peel. For 42 years she had been in charge of Knockaloe's poultry section but this was about to be wound down so she was given responsibility instead for the cattery. She had two Manx cats of her own so had an interest in them.

There were real fears that Manx cats were beginning to die out, she said. It was thought that their bowel problems might be because of too much inbreeding among domestic cats so it was decided to toughen up the variety by bringing in the blood of males with a strong independent streak, many of them drawn from farms. Sometimes their origins were unknown but pedigrees were unimportant. What mattered was that they displayed the distinctive features of a Manx and were sturdy creatures.

"Cats who have had to fend for themselves are usually stronger than hand fed toms," she said.

This proved to be the case when cat 'flu swept through the cattery. It was a severe outbreak but all survived.

By the autumn of 1962 the cattery had 14 residents. Founder members included a black and white queen called Mitzi and three toms, Blackie, Jinx and (the pride of them all) the pure white Snowy.

Two recruits were tortoiseshell kittens found on the brooghs overlooking the old fishyard at Peel. Local postman Arthur Gill told Mrs Teare he had seen the kittens running about the brooghs. Armed with a net, she tracked them down to a hole beneath a stone wall. The only way to get them out was to reach in. That resulted in a well punctured and bloodied hand which took a while afterwards to heal but Mrs Teare always thought it worth it. "They produced some really beautiful kittens," she said.

Her secret for taming semi-feral kittens? "Keep them on the hungry side - then feed them. They'll be docile in a couple of weeks."

The two from the brooghs proved to be long-lived. One survived to 16; the other, 17. On taking them home, however, there was one moment when Mrs Teare felt like murdering them.

They got out of a box in which she was keeping them and fled up a chimney, fell down covered in soot and promptly clawed their way up her curtains! "I wasn't best pleased just then, I can tell you," she said.

Being remote from traffic and people the cattery could afford to operate a relaxed regime. Whilst there were special pens for the resident cats they were permitted to wander the nearby fields where they could indulge their hunting instincts.

None ever wandered too far, however. Life at the cattery was too comfortable. Every day Mrs Teare rode by motor scooter to Knockaloe to provide meals which the cats adored. Usually the meals included cuts from carcasses obtained by Mr Kerruish from the local abattoir which had been condemned as being unfit for human consumption. One speciality was sheep's brains.

Mrs Teare used to rattle a bucket and the cats would come running. "It was a wonderful sight," she said.

Cattery policy was to cook meals for young cats but the older ones had their meat raw.

By the summer of 1963 the number of adult cats was 20; this despite another outbreak of flu' which killed two of the breeding toms.

Numbers were increasing so it was considered safe to sell kittens. Thus commenced an export policy. It was contradictory to the original nature of the place but would be pursued throughout the remainder of the cattery's history. The first kittens went to France, the U.S.A. and Canada, their pedigree name that of Mannanagh.

The Board of Agriculture had an understandable pride in the venture: its publicity impact quite beyond the scale of operation. Its pride was reflected in the adoption of a tabby Manx cat called Maisie as the indefinite illustration on the cover of

the Board's seasonal publication for farmers: the "Manx Journal of Agriculture."

For breeding purposes the situation was perfect. For public accessibility it was poor.

Originally the latter had not been considered. But now that a cattery existed whenever tourists or VIPs visiting the Island said they hadn't seen a Manx cat they were told, usually by Tourist Board staff: Go to Knockaloe.

Now more people visited Knockaloe to see the cats than did to see all the other demonstrations and facilities on agriculture that were available. Among them were visiting T.V. crews.

In one fortnight in August 1963 600 people did so, despite the experimental farm being remote and unsuited for visitors.

Thus it was that the idea occurred: This could become a show-piece; an attraction in itself. But not at Knockaloe. The Tourist Board believed it was necessary to "bring the cats to an audience than the audience to the cats." Inspired by this, Douglas Corporation made a decisive offer: If Knockaloe transferred the cattery to Douglas the town would build an appropriate place in Noble's Park where the breeding could continue and people could see the cats more easily.

SO *it* happened. The Board of Agriculture's Manx Journal of Agriculture gained a Hereford bull on its front cover in place of Maisie the cat. Douglas gained its first Municipal cats.

The cattery cost the Corporation £2,500 in set-up expenses. There were special pens and sleeping boxes for

Yes! I am a cat of the Manx,
And therefore escape silly pranks,
Not having a tail,
The naughty boys fail,
To swing me around: many thanks!

Kys ta Shiu?

Ellan Vannin

Douglas Cattery admission ticket

the "residents" and a kitchen where the keeper could make meals twice a day. Pedigrees were displayed in a viewing corridor for visitors which ran the full length of one side of the building.

Alderman Bill Kaneen ventured the thought that this could be the nucleus of a children's zoo, again a further departure from the original concept.

Because the cats at Knockaloe were able to wander at will the "round-up" for the transfer to Douglas took two days. Most, including Number 1 tom "Fearless Fred", were brought by car to Noble's Park on July 27th 1964 by Government Vet Douglas Kerruish and Douglas Gardens Superintendant Eric Coward but two couldn't be found and had to be collected the next day. A day later the cattery was opened to the public though a formal official opening didn't occur until August.

The first kitten, Shanie, was born on August 9th. Thereafter kittens were offered for sale at £7.75p each plus carriage. Prospective purchasers were required to complete application forms at the cattery.

Eventually the demand rose to such an extent that the waiting list reached an estimated six years. It was such an impossible situation that the old system was abandoned. Instead, applications for kittens were limited to one season only and had to be renewed annually if they couldn't be satisfied.

From the outset the cattery's new location meant that more people saw Manx cats: on average about thirty-five thousand people a year. It was the only place of its kind in the world, they were told.

Some trusted visitors were allowed a hands-on experience, given cats to stroke and cuddle and kittens to feed. One visitor had to be sponged down after a kitten was sick down his trousers and over his shoes but incidents like that were rare.

Occasionally visiting drunks caused problems. One Scotsman squeezed a cat so firmly that it screamed and left the man covered in scratches but he could scarce complain.

When certain cats had litters they were inclined to bite and warning notices sometimes went unheeded. Children stuck fingers through netting, disturbed cats and were bitten. But again neither the offenders nor their parents could complain. They had been warned.

Only one situation proved to be a problem: the tendency for an old tabby tom called Odin to turn his back on visitors he disliked and spray them - sometimes from the far side of the cattery!

No one complained, however. They knew it was the sort of risk they took when visiting a cattery.

Here's a MANX CAT

With Greetings

THE MANX CATTERY
Douglas · Isle of Man

From souvenir note-pad.

Controversy, when it occurred, didn't concern the cats; more the conditions in which they were housed.

Many cat-lovers didn't like the cramped quarters, particularly the absence of an outdoor run. After being allowed to roam free at Knockaloe the cats must have found the cattery to be like a prison. Then, being in such a busy and public place there had to be greater security.

In response to criticisms, that December there was less cageing. On alternate days the male cats were allowed to roam free in the visitors' passage with females not in kitten or with kitten.

It was a risk, especially when a window was broken - and on May 23rd 1965 the two year old light brown striped Tiger made a dash for freedom. He got clean away through the window - but despite what the critics said, life at the cattery couldn't have been all that bad for next day he came back of his own accord!

Later another tom was allowed to roam free around the park and could always be relied upon to return.

Still the criticisms persisted. The Manx Society for the Prevention of Cruelty to Animals condemned the cattery as being "anything but good."

Later there were calls for grassed enclosed runs to be provided so the cats were not kept indoors all the time; then, when the Corporation refused to oblige, the chief vet of the R.S.P.C.A. was called in.

His findings actually favoured the Corporation. The cats were in sound health and condition, he said, and did not appear to suffer from any deprivation through being prevented from going outside. Whilst outdoor runs would be a welcome addition to the cattery they were not essential. Cats could get along well enough without them.

The M.S.P.C.A. maintained its hostility even so. Subsequently, a society officer Bob Teare claimed that the cats were being over-bred and their diet was unsatisfactory. If people wanted to see Manx cats in satisfactory conditions they should visit the Association's headquarters at Ard Jerkyl where strays were kept. To prevent over-breeding and to ensure the future protection of the Manx breed the M.S.P.C.A. suggested that a Manx Cat Breeding Society should be formed. However, subsequent Gardens Superintendent Peter Dunn denied allegations of over-breeding. How could anyone make such suggestions without reference to the breeding records? he wondered.

Still, the M.S.P.C.A. maintained its criticisms. Grass might be grown in pots in the cattery so the cats could chew it but cat lovers didn't think it was enough. In 1974, the same year as the cattery provided cats for an appearance on B.B.C. TV's "Blue Peter," the M.S.P.C.A. condemned the place as "an unhygienic prison." Calling for it to be closed down, it said: Breeding Manx cats there was just a publicity stunt.

Sensitive to international publicity along these lines, Douglas Corporation's Parks Committee called in veterinary experts, was advised that the cattery was indeed unsatisfactory but rather than close it, Councillors

refurbished it, adding enclosed runs at one side as well as fitting a new ventilation system.

Cat lovers who visited the place thereafter and signed a Visitors' Book seemed well satisfied. Almost all comments indicated pleasure at what they had seen.

There was just one exception.

Curiously, no one gave any thought to the creation of a place where mating cats could have privacy. There was a small isolation pen where sick cats could be placed or new recruits kept for a required fortnight's quarantine before being introduced to the others but this was too small for anything else but that.

Mrs Sheila Quaggin, one of those responsible for running the cattery, recalled later: "What we had to do for decency's sake when two cats were together and there were so many people visiting the place was hang up a few blankets to hide them."

Thereafter the criticisms were more muted.

In the end the decisive issue did not concern conditions but the harsh one of economics.

By 1988 the cattery was losing the Corporation an estimated £9,000 a year. There weren't enough paying visitors or sales of kittens. The cost of each kitten born was put at between £360 and £700 each, depending on how the calculations were made! Not all kittens survived, after all. Some had to be put down because of physical deformities at birth.

The reaction by Councillors was to privatise the operation, the lessees taking over responsibility for the cats. One lessee lasted a year; another, not quite two.

There were proposals then to form a Friends of the Cattery organisation, to enable people interested in the Manx cat to become involved in running the place. Some people had given their cats on loan for breeding and liked to visit the cattery occasionally to see how their puss was progressing. Perhaps this interest could be extended, it was thought. However, the plan was overtaken by events.

In February 1992 Councillors, tired of all the aggravation it had caused, decided that the cattery would have to close. It wasn't viable as a commercial concern, they said; nor was it an effective tourist attraction. That its original purpose had been neither; that the concept had been more of an ark where a rare cat variety which had become a symbol of the Island could be preserved, had been forgotten. Town Clerk Don Peers simply observed: "It just seems as if people don't want to see cats in the cattery any more. We have lost an awful lot of money over the years."

So ended the Island's official involvement with Manx cats, its residents "retired" to good homes in the countryside.

Some welcomed its demise. Marjorie Joughin - formerly a senior member of the M.S.P.C.A. - condemned it as "the Battery Cattery."

Yet not all were pleased.

One breeder who wasn't was Sylvia Church whose cattery in St Paul's Cray near Orpington in Kent is known as Traa dy Liooar. In Manx that means 'Time enough.' "I've time enough for Manxies," she explains. Sylvia had to wait two years to get her first Manx kitten from the cattery. Later she bought the last to be sold by it - Dhooish, a male with big haunted eyes.

The tragedy of the cattery's closure, she said, was that "now there is no home-based central reference point for the breed."

Exports

* Kittens exported by the Cattery included a breeding pair sold for £7.35p each in 1970 to the then Minister of Petroleum and Natural Resources in Saudi Arabia. From Douglas the kittens were despatched in wooden boxes to Ronaldsway Airport, taken to London and from there to the Middle East. The operation took no more than 24 hours; the cost for transport, £24.

* One of the most unusual requests from a buyer came in June 1974. A woman in Droitwich, Staffs wanted to make a gift of two rumpy kittens to the town of Gabrovo in Bulgaria. If she paid for them, she asked, would the cattery fund their travel costs? Initially the Corporation's Parks Committee agreed but at a Town Council meeting it was ruled that it was a wrong use of ratepayers' money.

The cats made it to Bulgaria though. A local travel agency, Mann Travel, undertook to fly the kittens there free of charge.

* Probably the most dramatic sale occurred towards the end of the cattery's life. A couple had arrived to collect their kitten but he had been stung on a paw by a bee. One of the staff rushed to a nearby house, got a raw onion and smeared its juice onto the painful paw. Later Mrs Sheila Quaggin said the homeopathic remedy worked well.

Closure of the cattery meant that concern for the future of the Manx cat on the Isle of Man re-focussed on the activities of the M.S.P.C.A.

Questions were asked like: Was its activities over feral cat colonies threatening the gene pool?

In 1995 there were a number of established colonies: notably one in North Ramsey near the Grand Island Hotel, one in the south at Port St Mary and one at Cronk-y-Voddy. Whilst the majority of the cats in them were tailed they had a history of producing rumpies. Hence the concern by cat lovers over an M.S.P.C.A. policy (in line with that of the Cats Protection League and the U.K.'s R.S.P.C.A.) of catching them in baited traps every so often, neutering them (including rumpies) at the society's base in Ard Jerkyl, Foxdale and then releasing them back into the wild after three or four days.

The Ellan Vannin Cat Protection Trust which receives into its care feral cats found in obscure places like old tips also neuters all adult cats before finding them homes.

Critics warned that this would reduce the gene pool, therefore the number of tailless cats that occur naturally. This could threaten the rumpy's long-term survival as a naturally-occurring cat. The M.S.P.C.A., however, refused to accept that.

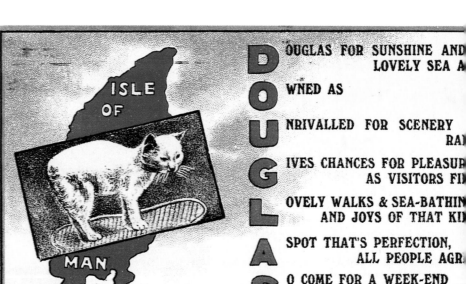

"The cats won't die out because of our policy," said Animal Welfare Officer Judy Corrin. "We have such a large cat population we'd be overrun by them if we didn't do something. It'd be impossible to home them all."

Significantly the policy does not apply to kittens so the potential bearers of a new generation of Manx escape. Every year some pregnant and homeless Manxies are brought into Ard Jerkyl. Demand for their rumpy kittens is constant so there are no problems in placing them. They are adopted, free of charge, once they are between eight to nine weeks old and that's too young for neutering. The society doesn't neuter any cat under six months old.

According to M.S.P.C.A. rules the kittens cannot be exported either so they are retained for the Island and help to preserve the gene pool. That's despite Ard Jerkyl receiving enquiries from all over the world about the availability of Manx cats. Breeders and cat lovers would pay good prices for its kittens but it isn't society policy to cater for that demand, lucrative though it could be. The society is concerned only with finding good and suitable homes for their charges on the Island.

"If we allowed kittens

to leave the Island," says Judy, "we'd have no way of knowing where they are going and how they will be treated."

Dr. Larch Garrad of the Manx Museum isn't particularly concerned about the future of the Manx cat. For two years at the end of the 1970s an American geneticist conducted a population survey on the Island, going from house to house, particularly in local authority estates, asking if they had a cat and, if so, was it a Manx. The result showed that perhaps one in ten or one in eleven were Manx: enough, said Dr Garrad, to remove the Manx from any list of endangered species.

M.S.P.C.A. *vet Stuart Angus* reached the same conclusion in 1995. Initially he had noticed a reduction in the ratio of Manx cats to normal ones attending veterinary surgeries. It was evidence which, taken in isolation, supported renewed fears that the Manx cat population was in decline. However, there was a broader picture to be considered, he said. "I don't think there has been a decline in numbers; rather, an increase in the number of other cats on the Island as the cat has become the most popular pet."

This verdict supports casual observations since then which suggest that the population has risen in line with that of humans.

Greetings from the Isle of Man

The Manx – American connection

When Carl Weigant of New York and Joe Rummler of Chicago - two undergraduates of Cornell University - crossed the Atlantic in 1929 in a 46ft 12-ton ketch they wanted a souvenir of their achievement.

Their choice? A tailless Manx kitten.

In October that year, as they planned a return trip across the Atlantic via the Azores and West Indies in December or January, they travelled to the Isle of Man and acquired the required cat.

Thus was demonstrated the on-going love affair North Americans have had for the Manx cat.

Today there are probably more Manx cats in the U.S.A. and Canada than in their place of origin. There are numerous breeders and at least two small magazines to serve them have been published: "Manx World," published in the 1960s as the journal of the International Manx Cat Society, based in Wisconsin, Canada and "The Manx Cat" - "dedicated to the welfare and continued improvement of the purebred Manx from the Isle of Man" - published in Illinois in the 1980s.

Between them they have spread knowledge of the Isle of Man and its geography throughout America more than anything else. Many breeders name their businesses after place names on the Island and the majority of their cats too. Maybe some have difficulty with the pronunciation of them but that doesn't deter. Rather, it probably adds to the fascination; the awareness that here is something different to the normal.

In June 1973 Manx cats were reported to be "running wild" in New York.

An astonished Manx visitor - Mrs Pat Bagg (wife of a former principal keeper at the Calf of Man Lighthouse) - said she had seen at least twelve tailless cats running loose in the city. Her cousin had taken in a stray Manx cat too and nursed it back to health.

Incredible? Not necessarily.

Like the Irish, Manx people emigrated to North America in great numbers in the early part of the 19th century and they brought their cats with them.

The first recorded Manx cat immigrant was in 1820.

Inevitably the tailless gene found its way into the continent's feline population - concentrated in some parts, more diluted elsewhere.

In the Blue Ridge Mountains of Virginia there are tailless feral cats known locally as Bobtails but Manx-born Sally Black who lived nearby said there was no doubt about it - they were Manx.

Manx cats reverting to the wild was probably the explanation for what happened in the mid-1980s near the Florida Everglades at Orlando. A tailless kitten was found among some rubbish. For a local county attorney who was given it the cat was her introduction to the Isle of Man and eventually she came to the Island to investigate the cat's origins.

Other rumpies have found their way to the U.S.A. through cat-lovers and breeders importing them from the Isle of Man. Americans have been the keenest buyers this century, some travelling to the Island from the States just to make a purchase.

Why the interest?

In 1954 John Gould of Maine, the owner of a cat called Stubbie (the latest in a long succession of Manx cats owned by him) gave a tongue in cheek explanation to the Christian Science Monitor.

Taillessness was a distinct asset in a Maine winter, he said. A cat without a tail could pass through an open door much quicker than a tailed one!

"During the rigours of a Maine winter that's not to be laughed at," he added.

Getting accustomed to quicker exits and entries, however, did have its disadvantages.

When a long-tailed stray was given a home, Mr Gould's Aunt Abigail failed to allow for the tail when closing the door. It crunched on the cat's tail and the usually placid kitten was transformed into a ferocious wild thing - racing up one side of Aunt Abigail and down the other with appropriate remarks all round.

Ever since, said Mr Gould, he'd stuck to short-tailed cats or rumpies.

Throughout North America there are an estimated 100 breeders specialising in Manx cats.

According to British breeder Freda Williams of the Dreemskerry Manx Cattery in Hampshire, who has toured America with her own show cats, the best Manx cats in the world, apart from an odd specimen on the Isle of Man (which nine times out of ten are unregistered) are to be found down the Californian coast. "They really do have some beautiful ones," she says.

It is in California that the club Manx International is based. It claims members throughout the world, notably from America, Canada, Australia, New Zealand, Holland and Germany.

Mrs Jessie Twining of Greeba, Isle of Man, the Island's most prominent Manx cat breeder of the 1940s and '50s, was the breeder who exported Mrs Kelly of An-Si to the States in 1952, the buyer being Mrs Anne Bieneman of Pittsburgh. The cat became known as "Mrs Kelly, the perfect cat," and was featured on television and in the National Geographic magazine. She was the first cat to become Grand and Quadruple Champion of all-America in two successive years - in 1955 and 1956.

Another outstanding Manx-American cat was Manninagh Mona of Mount Snaefell.

Born at the Knockaloe Cattery just before it was moved to Douglas in 1964, she was bought by Mr and Mrs William Bryan who had a cattery at Hatboro, Pennsylvania and had come to the Isle of Man specially for the purchase. Her name was chosen at a

Clácritter Lyla from the U.S.A.

lunch in Ramsey with Government Vet Douglas Kerruish. The Bryans considered her "the finest the Island had to offer," a judgement confirmed by Mona's subsequent show successes in America. In the next 11 years she won more than 1,200 awards at shows in America and Canada.

Later Mr and Mrs Bryan acquired more cats from the Isle of Man; they even came and judged local Manx cats at the Royal Manx Agricultural Show in 1969 but they always maintained: Mona was the most intelligent cat they had come across. She could remember judges from show to show and would take up statuesque poses for them, drawing herself to full height, rump up, head high and looking straight ahead. "She seemed to enjoy the 'Oohs' and 'Aahs' of the audience," said Mr Bryan.

She used to sit, well behaved, on a table too when Mr and Mrs Bryan gave lectures on Manx cats. Afterwards she responded well to fusses from the audience.

On June 5th 1976 when Mona was 12 years old the Bryans held a special birthday party for her at Hatboro. Foremost in their thoughts then was the memory that she nearly never made it to the States.

Somewhere between PanAm accepting her and her scheduled delivery to Mr and Mrs Bryan's cattery, Mona disappeared. It was only after the police had been called in to help search for her and many transatlantic telephone calls later that Mona was located.

Every year more Americans join Japanese and others in pilgrimages to the Island to buy Manx cats direct from local breeders.

One who did so in 1994 was so delighted with her cat that she arranged a special surprise for breeder, Mrs Sheila Quaggin of Ballakayt Manx, 145 Woodbourne Road, Douglas. Early in 1995 Mrs

MANX CATS CROSS THE ATLANTIC

AMERICANS AND CANADIANS FALL FOR THE TAILLESS BREED

Some Remarkable Show Successes

from the 'Ramsey Courier' 15 . III . 57

Quaggin was surprised to receive a request from the Post Office to collect a special package it had received from the White House in Washington D.C.

What could it be? she wondered. On opening it she found it to be a picture of President Clinton's cat, Socks. Apparently it was in return for him receiving a picture of the Manx kitten bred by Sheila and now an American resident.

It was probably a cat from one of the many American Manx cat breeders who supplied the cat that surprised Douglas Gardens Superintendant Peter Dunn whilst on a holiday to

Florida in 1991. Visiting botanic gardens on the west coast he encountered a black and white tailless tom wandering free.

Former pets who have succumbed to a Manx cat's independent streak and deserted their owners are another explanation for the sudden and apparently inexplicable appearance of tailless kittens in litters.

One Manx cat wanderer called Shady "adopted" Port Hueneme City Hall (near Thousand Oaks, California) in the mid-1980s. For many years thereafter he roamed the corridors and meeting rooms of City Hall - even making an unauthorised entry into the Council chamber during a meeting!

In August 1987 when a particularly severe tornado swept through the Canadian prairies rescuers discovered a little black tailless kitten wandering aimlessly. Eventually, according to the Edmonton Journal, she was found to be the sole survivor of a litter of Manxies in a trailer park devastated by the tornado. Her name was "B.J." (short for Bear Junior). She was the pet of a young mother and her eleven week old baby, both badly injured when their trailer collapsed.

Two North American Manxies who hit the headlines in the early 1930s were Amos and Andy.

Named after popular American comedians of the period, they were the pets of Mrs N. L. Bissonette of Timmins, Ontario, Canada.

She was given them by her brother in 1933 and by the following year they had earned themselves a place in the Denver Post as the cats who loved to eat cigarettes, tobacco and soap.

"They were the most peculiar kittens I have ever seen," she said. "Amos immediately took to eating every cigarette-end he could find and if ever a tobacco pouch was lying around he would scratch it open and eat the tobacco.

"Andy developed different tastes entirely. He refused to eat anything that Amos would eat. He was fond of beer and if he ever missed his beer he would upset ink bottles and lap up ink."

It was Amos who was fond of soap. "Every morning my husband was shaving," said Mrs Bissonette, "he would climb up his shoulder and lick the lather off his face. We thought this great fun."

One thing he didn't like was onions. See one in Mrs Bissonette's hands and he would rush outdoors.

Sadly, one day he never returned.

Knowing of her association with the Isle of Man, the owner of the Manx kittens offered one to her and she accepted. "I never thought that one day I would get a Manx cat in America," she said.

He grew up to be a big and tough individual, strong enough to overcome an accident with a truck which cost him his teeth on one side the mouth.

Then came the novel twist.

In 1993 Sally and her husband decided to move to Castletown in the Isle of Man and take over an antique shop, Antiquarium, in Malew Street.

Ramsey had to come with them, they decided, despite a six month quarantine in Liverpool - and their long-tailed pet Ronague too.

And so he did.

Very soon he became one of the characters of the town, strutting around the old market square, posing for photographers and allowing himself to be petted, so Manx in his

appearance that no one could guess that he was really American-born. In America he had been accustomed to the freedom of five acres of farmland. Here, despite the dangers of traffic, Sally and her husband allowed him the freedom to wander at will and town's people quickly came to look upon him as a character. Sometimes he'd wander into the local branch of Barclay's Bank for a cat-nap, occasionally the hairdressing shop. He earned a reputation too for wailing outside the fishmonger's until a tasty morsel was given him.

Said Sally later: "Everyone so likes him I guess they'll give him a state funeral when he dies."

American - Manxie 'Ramsey' has a good stretch at Castletown. Photo courtesy Sally and Steve Black.

Probably the most curious story of a Manx cat is that of Ramsey. He became the American Manxie who eventually found his roots.

The yellow-eyed black and white rumpy was born in 1989 in Charlottesville, Virginia, one of a litter of nine, all Manx.

Sally Black, formerly of Port St Mary and a lover of Manx cats all her life, was living nearby with her husband Steve. She was a book illustrator and he an art director for scientific books.

This is how some American Manx cat lovers celebrated the achievements of a rumpy.

They produced a commemorative plate.

It was made by the Kettlesprings Kilns Alliance in Ohio in 1962 and went on display at Chicago's Third International Folk Fair at the Navy Pier later that year.

The plate was designed by Mrs Alexander Ebin (otherwise known by her maiden Manx name of Dorothy Mylrea) and was sold as a fund-raiser for the North American Manx Association's Convention which was to be held in Chicago in 1963.

The transfer print depicts international champion Manx cat, and founder of a line of outstanding champions, the red tabby Ginger of Manx of Glen Orry, a cattery based in the rural west of Chicago. Ginger is shown playing the favourite Manx song "Ellan Vannin" on a piano. He was born in the Isle of Man, exported to Denmark and then imported from there into the U.S.A. in 1935.

Manx cats owned by Ruth and Ellen Carlson of Glen Orry, breeders since 1933 and organisers of annual Manx cat shows in Chicago, were a popular attraction at the Folk Fair. They included a red Manx tabby called Olaf who was the best male cat in the U.S.A. in 1960/61.

A black haired successor whose ancestry was traceable to Ginger had a phenomenal run of show successes. Toshee's name meant 'leading' or 'foremost' - an appropriate choice for she won the American Cat Fanciers award of "Kitten of the Year," and by 1972 was described as "pretty close to perfection."

In that year she competed in 37 shows and won best cat award in 25 of them.

Another descendant of Ginger was the champion Jerry, owned by Harry Lyndes of Denver, Colorado. In 1949 he achieved show successes all over America.

Manx cats hit the San Franciscan headlines in 1952 when the North American Manx Society was holding its Convention there.

All-American triple champion Nani Lei Lady Red Moire and her four month old son, Nani Lei Bob All Red, owned by Mildred Joseph of Castro Valley, were brought onto a live T.V. chat show broadcast by KRON-TV, sponsored by the San Francisco Herald and dealing with the Convention. Then "Mum" broke her leash and dashed for freedom, desperately followed by her son. "Mum" disappeared under some scenery and the scene ended with a Manx-American woman on her hands and knees trying to induce the cat to come out.

Eventually order was restored - but only temporarily.

Later at the Whitcomb Hotel, which was being used as the headquarters for the Manx Convention, "Mum" cat broke free again and dashed outside. She ended up in an alley, under a building, and only emerged when her son was brought to her in a cage.

"Lady Red came out as swiftly as a girl who'd lived in alleys all her life," said the San Francisco Chronicle next day, "shot across to a parked car and slid up onto a tyre under a front fender. And like an alley girl, she bit and scratched when the forces of respectability took hold."

The story was published under the title of "A Manx Cat flees and thereby hangs a tale."

* KIRRY Teare, a Manx cat from Marathon Road, Douglas was better behaved when she appeared on T.V. Though sick on the plane which took her to the B.B.C. studios in Birmingham several years after the American incident, she performed well - and enjoyed all the fussing she received from studio staff.

"SLAYNT AS SHEA AS AASH DY VEA AS MARRYNS SON DY BRAGH"

"HEALTH AND PEACE AND LENGTH OF DAYS AND HAPPINESS FOR EVER"

NAMA VICTORY CONVENTION

Postcard issued at the North American Association Convention held in Toronto and dated 8 . VIII . 47.

Beauty and the Gorilla

In June 1984 a mighty lowland gorilla called Koko received an extra special present. It was a pet to love and care for . . . a Manx rumpy kitten!

She cuddled and caressed it gently with arms and fingers which so easily could have crushed it to death. Then later she did the same with another rumpy then a rumpy riser.

The display of gentleness captured on film by America's non-profitmaking Gorilla Foundation subsequently captured the public's imagination. A colour poster produced and sold on behalf of the Foundation's funds by the National Geographic Magazine proved to be a major seller.

Later came a book, "Koko and her kittens," which was popular among American schools.

Dr Francine (Penny) Patterson, editor of the Gorilla Journal, kept a record of Koko's developing relationships. She wrote later: "It surprises most people that a gorilla could be so gentle with such tiny, helpless creatures, but information on both wild and captive gorillas indicates this to be consistent with the gorilla temperament."

In 1941 a book called "Toto and I"

written by Maria Hoyt described how a gorilla called Toto adopted a black and white kitten. Later in Rwanda a gorilla was found petting a baby antelope and at San Francisco Zoo sparrow-hawks which escaped from a nearby unit were caught by gorillas and stroked by them for several minutes.

Born in 1971 and raised at San Francisco's Children's Zoo, Koko displayed that same gentleness with a cat owned by the zoo's director and known as Barney Google. Because of this she became a candidate a year later for an exercise in inter-species communications code-named "Project Koko." This was started in a compound at Stanford University by PhD candidate Francine Patterson, one of the founders with Dr Ronald Cohn and the late Barbara Hiller in 1976 of the Gorilla Foundation, the world's first organisation dedicated to the support and preservation of gorillas and which now has a membership of over 60,000.

The aim of the project was to study gorilla intelligence and, whilst gorillas are physically incapable of speech, to establish a means of communication through the development of a vocabulary of signs.

As Koko grew older and the project was transferred to the forested highlands of Woodside, California where a more protected environment could be provided, this progressed beyond all expectations. She acquired a working vocabulary of over 500 signs, an understanding of 400 more and about 2,000 words of spoken English. Her IQ was tested at between 70 and 95 on a human scale.

A male gorilla, two years her junior,

Manx Cat

called Michael - acquired in 1976 for similar instruction and as a possible mate for Koko in future - developed many communicating skills too.

It *was* using the sign language on July 1st 1983 that Koko's teachers told her that they wanted to give her a present for her twelfth birthday then asked: What did she want?

No doubt remembering a cat which one of her teachers had brought to her earlier, Koko replied: "Cat."

A black and white stray had been given to Koko whilst at San Francisco Zoo. It was named K.C., short for "Koko's Cat." However, when Koko was relocated to Stanford the cat vanished, never to be seen again.

Now Koko wanted a replacement.

A small plastic toy one was obtained for her. Then, as Christmas approached, Francine produced a small hand-drawn catalogue of possible gifts that she had produced, showed it to Koko and asked what did she want for Christmas? Koko pointed to drawings of a doll, some nuts and a cat.

All three were provided, the cat in

the form of a realistic life-sized one, but Koko was upset and did two display charges. Later she was seen kissing the cat and rubbing it with her cheek (the agreed sign for "soft").

It was decided then that one day soon a real cat should be given to her.

No one feared for its safety. Francine said later: The Foundation believed that all living things, from the smallest kitten to the largest gorilla, should be treated with care and kindness. "We would never, under any circumstances, consider giving to Koko any animal which we did not feel would benefit from the relationship."

Five months later a litter of kittens, one of them a Manx tom, was born to a cat owned by one of the researchers, Karen Gallinetti. They had been abandoned by the mother and nursed instead by a Cairn terrier.

Here was Koko's chance, it was decided.

When four weeks old the kittens were brought to Koko in a box by Karen and shown to her one by one. After she had blown on each one Koko was asked: Which one did she want? and she pointed to the rumpy.

It was a particularly fascinating choice for it was a Manx privateer and slave trader, William Lace (1763-1850), who was credited in Britain with bringing the first news of gorillas from Africa.

Also, for the first time a real-life gorilla denied one of the lines in Symbolic Logic written in 1896 by Lewis Carroll, author of Alice in Wonderland. "No kitten without a tail will play with a gorilla," he wrote.

Well, now one did.

For a short while Koko was allowed to play with all the kittens which she did with great gentleness. The rumpy was carried on Koko's thigh then on the back of her neck; then she cradled him, examined his paws and squeezed them to reveal his claws.

Afterwards, when all the kittens were returned to their box, Koko signed to Karen: "Cat do scratch Koko - love."

Two days later the Manx rumpy was brought back and Koko was asked to name him. Her decision was "All Ball," an appropriate name everyone decided because, minus a tail, the kitten looked like a ball of fur.

Three days later Koko played with All Ball on her stomach and near her breast. Asked what she was laughing about she replied: "Soft tiger cat. Nipple gorilla tickle."

After subsequent playing together Koko was asked: "Do you love Ball?"

Despite All Ball having developed a tendency to bite, Koko replied: "Soft, good cat."

"Is Ball fun?" she was asked and Koko observed: "Teeth there . . . !"

Tragedy intervened one rainy day just before Christmas 1984.

All Ball managed to escape through a door which had been opened to let in dogs for a meal and failed to respond to his name being called. At first it was hoped that he would shelter beneath a nearby trailer and return when he was hungry. But he didn't.

Later it was discovered that he had been knocked down and killed by a passing car.

When told what had happened Koko didn't reply immediately then a few minutes later gave the tearless hooting cry of a gorilla.

Koko was still mourning for her cat some days later when she was asked if she wanted to talk about All Ball. Koko gave the sign for "Cry."

"What happened to your kitty?" she was asked.

She signed: "Sleep cat."

"Yes, he's sleeping," she was told whereupon Koko signed: "Koko good."

Public reaction to the news of Koko's bereavement was unprecedented. Letters of sympathy flooded in to the Gorilla Foundation; even children's drawings of crude Manx cats. There were phone calls too offering new cats.

That a gorilla could establish such a relationship and grieve so touched people deeply.

Said one woman in a letter to Koko: "I cried when I read it. I read it in the night and cried myself to sleep. I'm really sorry because you loved the kitten so much..."

Later, asked what she would like for Christmas again, Koko signed: "Cat, cat, tiger cat."

It was hoped at first that All Ball's mother might oblige with another litter and maybe another Manx but that didn't occur.

On March 17th 1985, after further requests by Koko for another cat, Francine showed Koko drawings of three cats, one with a tail, a stumpy and a rumpy. What kind would she like? she was asked and Koko pointed to the rumpy.

Then she would get one, she was told. Was that O.K.?

"Good, nice," signed Koko.

Later in that same session Koko was asked about her feelings over losing All Ball.

"Want," she signed.

"Were you sad?" she was asked and Koko replied: "Frown lip visit bad, frown, frown - sad. Sorry."

Koko got her new pet Manx rumpy on the evening of March 23rd. The kitten had been donated by a local family.

On being shown him briefly Koko purred.

Next day Koko danced when the kitten was returned to her. She held the young tom close to her chest and purred more so when he meowed.

On subsequent visits she was asked to name the kitten and she settled on "Lips."

Why? she was asked.

She signed "Lipstick."

The reason then was self-evident. The kitten had a pink nose. Evidently, deduced Francine, Koko associated it with human lips.

Lips was introduced later to the male gorilla, Michael.

When asked what he thought of Koko's cat he replied: "My cat good." The emphasis on the "My," prompted everyone to conclude: When All Ball's mother had another litter, Koko could have her choice from those kittens then "Lips" could become Michael's cat.

That April more kittens were born, two of them rumpy risers.

At three weeks old they were taken to Koko and she was asked to choose one. Everyone expected the choice to be one of the rumpy risers, especially one with a slightly screwed tail, but to everyone's amazement Koko chose the runt, a black and white tailed cat.

Koko was given repeated choices to make sure until such time as the kittens were old enough to leave their mother and every time she chose the same one, giving the "baby" sign and kissing and stroking her.

When Koko was bereaved by the loss of her first Manx cat she received many drawings from American children of tailless cats (Photo: Gorilla Foundation).

"Surprise" was her choice of name.

"Lips" and "Surprise" were held up together and Koko was asked: Which one did she want as her very own cat?

Without hesitation she pointed to the runt.

That seemed conclusive enough; sufficient for Michael to be given "Lips" without any risk of trouble.

His chosen name for her was: "My Cat Red."

Koko's love of a Manx cat didn't fade, however. Her choice of "Surprise" didn't last.

Her heart was won eventually by one of the other kittens, the fluffy grey rumpy riser with a corkscrew tail which she called "Smoke."

Thus was another Manx cat recruited by the Gorilla Foundation, known to everyone eventually as "Smoky."

One of her favourite perches on early visits to Koko was on top of the gorilla's head!

In the next eight years "Smoky" became adored by everyone at the Foundation - developing her own sign language too: a raised front paw when she wanted to be fed.

Says the Gorilla Foundation: "Project Koko has proven the stereotyped image of gorillas as bloodthirsty, destructive monsters unequivocally false. Indeed, it has forced a re-examination of traditional thought regarding all animals. The project has shown that an animal can possess qualities that were previously considered exclusively human, such as thought processes, imagination and feelings."

**Right: KoKo and her Manx kitten.
Below: Dr Francine Patterson with Koko and her kitten. Her book: "Koko's Kitten" has sold to schools worldwide.
Elizabeth Snyder, a teacher from a West Virginia school, wrote to the Gorilla Foundation that Koko was a symbol to her students that all animals had feelings and need love and attention.
"When one student lost her kitten she told me over and over: 'I know how Koko feels.'"
From Malaysia came a letter giving the reaction of a class of five and six year olds at a school for the children of the Esso Oil Company's expatriate workers. Originally a teacher had intended using photographs in the book as visual aids for the letter of the week, 'K'. "As I read the title and showed the photographs during our regular read-aloud period," wrote Jim Mazzarella, "I was met with such a level of curiosity and interest that I had to start reading from the first page. That level of concentration continued on beyond our regular reading time until I could finish . . ."
Photos: Copyright, Ronald H. Cohn / The Gorilla Foundation, Woodside, California 94062.**

The Manx Cat has given its name even to a small weekly satirical newspaper, albeit a short-lived one. "The Manx Cat or Isle of Man Charivari", full of anecdotes, ballads and jokes, was published by professional actor and ex-patriate Irishman, Alfred Ormonde, of 14 North Quay, Douglas who had a tendency to break into verse when he wrote. The first one penny issue was published on August 16th, 1847; the last in June 1848.

Several amusing designs featuring Manx cats were used for the publication's masthead. The first included a rumpy seated with a pince-nez and captioned: "I am a native here and to the manner born." A more frequently used design incorporated the Three Legs emblem within a shield, a herring being roasted on a grid-iron above it and two top-hatted and smoking Manx cats supporting it.

The "Manxman", a weekly satirical paper published in the 1890s by James Hartley of Upper Church Street, Douglas, "written by Manxmen for Manxmen and devoted to the best interests of the Manx people," also featured a Manx cat astride its masthead, significantly not a rumpy but a stumpy. Included in the masthead also was the Manx proverb: "Let every herring hang by his own gills."

A subsequent magazine which was also humorous featured a Manx cat on its front cover, though to a lesser extent. Inevitably the character Punch dominated the artwork designed by local artist John Millar Nicholson. The magazine was the Manx Punch, published between 1885 and 1886 by G. W. Dawson of Union Mills, believed to have been a former printing foreman with the Manx Sun newspaper.

MANX   CAT,

QUOCUNQUE·JECERIS·STABIT.

VANNIN VEG VEEN

THE MAN X MAN

QUOCUNQUE JECERIS STABIT

A WEEKLY CRITICAL AND SATIRICAL PAPER

WRITTEN BY

MANXMEN FOR MANXMEN & DEVOTED TO THE BEST INTERESTS OF THE MANX PEOPLE.

"LET EVERY HERRING HANG BY HIS OWN GILLS"

TOWER OF REFUGE

Vol. 2.—No. 17.   SATURDAY, SEPTEMBER 21st, 1895.   [Registered at the General Post Office as a Newspaper.]   [ONE PENNY.

Opening doors was no problem for this particular rumpy - a pet kept at Peel, Isle of Man in the 1930s. Manx cartoonist "Dusty" Miller illustrated the trick thus: The cat would leap onto a door handle, cling there, then pull down the latch with a paw. In the days before cat flaps it must have been a useful ability: certainly better than sitting outside in the cold hoping for a plaintive miaow to be heard.

Earlier this century a Douglas chemist had a cat which could cling onto a rounded door knob and make it turn.

The U.S.A.'s Detroit News reported a similar habit in April 1933 by Minerva the Manx cat - a young, silky kitten "with a tail like a powder puff," owned by Mrs Morgan Douglas of Detroit. Every morning Minerva went upstairs and rattled the bedroom doorknob to waken the family! Abilities such as this are no surprise to Manx cat breeders. They say Manx cats have a high I.Q.

Through the eyes of a P.O.W.

The Isle of Man through German eyes in the final days of World War 1.

In the first drawing in 1918 a reclining three legged Celtic sea god Mannanan, after whom the Island was named, plays gently with a Manx cat which is free to roam. In the second, Mannanan clenches to him a hapless German prisoner who bids to be free.

During the war tens of thousands of enemy aliens were interned on the Island; the biggest camp at Knockaloe housing an estimated 35,000.

Internees were allowed to design and produce their own greetings cards for Christmas and other special occasions and these were sent to their families. Manx cats were incorporated in many designs; a clear indication of how close the cat was regarded as a symbol of the Island.

FROM THE CIVILIAN CAMP AT KNOCKALOE, ISLE OF MAN 1918

"With happy laughter I greet you New Year! You come bringing fulfilment and peace. You bring soft tunes into the wild songs. I open my arms, feel you approach and see many angels decorate your path with flowers, palm trees and laurels. In my joyous delight I see like a mirage, the proud large picture of home to which my greetings go which is the object of my longings"

THE ACCURSED ISLAND 1918.

"Greetings to you at the change of the year. From the distant man of stone from where the longing looked to you year after year. Where I only knew happiness through the praise of your deeds, your loving greetings and when after hard (serious) work, I creep into my bunk, forgetting all suffering, know that I happily trust that what I hope will come."

Puzzle cats of Man

A late Victorian or early Edwardian tourist souvenir tea service, believed to have been produced in Bohemia, featured a hidden Manx cat in its design.

"The Manxman. Where's the cat?" demanded a caption beneath a design depicting on a white glazed background a red-coated three-legged Manxman walking near a tree and followed by a legendary tailless Manx rooster.

The cat can be found among the tree's branches, its white body outlined by the shape of the branches.

Examples of the tea service, which included a sugar bowl in the shape of a cauldron, are now rare.

Equally so are cotton women's headscarves printed locally in black and white depicting that and other puzzles. These were produced on behalf of a local shop, Cottier and Cubbon of Victoria Street, Douglas, between 1875 and 1914.

A rather evil-looking and smirking Manxie dominated one chortling: "Ha! Ha! Ha! I'm the Manx cat that has eaten the canary." Hidden in his features were those of his master and mistress.

"Hi, Kelly! I'm a Manx cat. Find the Dicky Bird," was another puzzle. Presumably it was in the cat's stomach!

An excellent detailed drawing of a tabby Manx cat featured on another with the outline of a Manx historical character hidden in his belly. This is believed to have been issued in 1882.

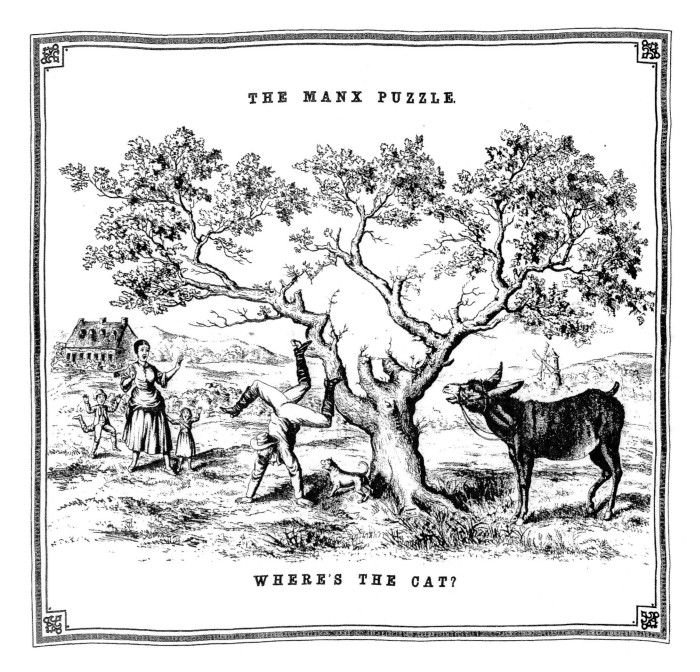

THE MANX PUZZLE.

WHERE'S THE CAT?

Humours of Manx History—No. 3

Why the Manxman has Three Legs

A three-legged man came mysteriously from the ground, followed by two rumpy cats and two ditto fowls. He said he was going to Paradise. But he met a Manx maid and found a Paradise on earth. They wed, and had thirteen sons all like father

So now you know all about it!

Note—Ben-my-Chree is Manx for "Girl of My Heart."

Copyright
Norris-Meyer Press

Going to the Shoe-Shine Shop in the Isle of Man.

By Gum! It's champion here.

Three-legged men, rumpies and tailless fowl were all curiosities for late Victorian and Edwardian visitors to the Isle of Man. The postcards to the left were published in the period 1904 – 1908; the one above, 1925. One writer in August 1908 says: "You have missed a treat. The place is crowded. We have met a lot of nice people."

The Louis Wain comic postcards

The Manx cat has been caricatured many times, especially for the traditional seaside postcard. Some of the artists are no longer known, but the name of one rings down through the decades . . .

It is that of Louis Wain, former artist with the Illustrated London News.

H.G.Wells, the author, said of him later that he "invented a cat style, a cat society, a whole cat world."

Ever since 1883 at the age of 23 Wain began to draw cats in human poses. Later Louis Wain annuals and comic postcards became big sellers. His interest in cats resulted in him being a judge at a cat show in the Royal Botanical Gardens (date unknown) when a Manx silver tabby kitten called Bonkaki (owned by the keeper of London Zoo) achieved the reputed distinction of being the first Manx cat to win a championship. The award was presented by the Princess of Wales, later Queen Alexandra.

Among Wain's huge output of cartoons was a small number about Manx cats in the Isle of Man, produced after 1904 and before the First World War in 1914. These are now highly collectable.

In later life the London-based Louis suffered from a mental illness which showed in the eyes of his cats and sometimes their frenzied activities but none of this was evident in his Manx cartoons. He died, hospitalised, in July 1939.

LouisWain.

CATCHING THE BOAT.

CAUGHT BY THE CAMERA IN MANXLAND.

A Wet Day on Board: Isle of Man

MIDNIGHT CONCERT

MANX KIPPERS FOR TEA.

A Fine Day on Board: Isle of Man

Louis Wain.

STORMY PASSAGE ON S. S. "VIKING"

Louis Wain.

On Coins and Stamps

Isle of Man coins and postage stamps have featured the Manx cat on a number of occasions since 1970.

Some coins have been so popular they have been enamelled and used as items of jewellery

The first coin to feature a Manx cat was a cupro-nickel Crown, issued in 1970. It appeared, however, only after royal criticism had resulted in a change of posture.

Vice-chairman of the Island's Finance Board, Clifford Irving, recalled later: "If the Queen's effigy is on a coin there is a committee at the Royal Mint which must approve the design. Apparently Prince Philip saw this one and said the cat didn't look virile enough."

Suitable amendments were made to make the posture more pleasing.

When a new set of Manx coinage was being planned for release in 1981 a Manx cat was incorporated as the main feature of the design of a penny coin. The coin was issued in bronze for general circulation but also in cupro-nickel, sterling silver, platinum and gold for collectors.

The minters were the privately-owned Pobjoy Mint in Sutton, Surrey.

Internationally, probably the most collected Manx cat coin was the gold bullion Crown issued in five different weights and with a limit of 4,300 sets in 1988. Since then it has been reported as having been traded at a premium.

The Crown was the first of a series of bullion Crowns struck in platinum and silver too on behalf of the Manx Government by the Pobjoy Mint and all featuring cats of the world. Others have included a New York alley cat.

The first Manx postage stamp to feature a rumpy was the 10p value in the first definitive set of stamps issued in July 1973.

John Nicholson, the Manx artist based at Spaldrick, Port Erin, who was to get into the Guinness Book of Records eventually as the designer of the most number of postage stamps for any one country, used his own pet cat Flopsy as the model, standing on a tree branch.

By the time a new definitive set was issued five years later in February 1978 Flopsy had died at the age of 16. Her son, Fred, however, was available as a model and as he loved catching lizards John was given permission by the Post Office Authority to include a small lizard in the stamp design.

A rumpy made an appearance along with a teddy bear and a child in the 5p Christmas stamp issued in 1979 which was designated The Year of the Child.

Manx cats were featured on a set of

1973 Manx stamp

1970 Manx Crown

1988 Manx Crown

1978 Manx stamp

four stamps designed by Guernsey-based artist Peter Layton and issued in February 1989. Postcards of the stamps were also published. The stamps, with face values of 16p, 27p, 30p and 40p, featured cats owned by Manx families. People were invited to submit photographs to the Post Office Authority and the four best were selected.

The rumpy on the 27p stamp proved to be one of the most filmed cats of the 1980s and 1990s - Tosca, the black and white pet of Doug Baird, later of the Tourist Department's press office. Doug's eleven year old daughter, Nicola, submitted the photograph to the Post Office.

When visiting TV film crews asked to see a Manxie, Doug found it easier to show them his own rather than take them round the Island. As a result, Tosca featured in more than twenty international TV documentaries. The 1989 set of stamps can be seen on the inside back cover.

In February 1994 a set of 'Happy Holiday' stamps featuring the Island's historic links with tourism depicted a Manx tabby in the foreground of a picture of Laxey water wheel.

Then in October that year a white-pawed tabby appeared in two of a series of six 'Postman Pat' stamps which imagined that the children's storybook favourite had visited the Island with his black and white cat Jess.

The 20p value stamp pictured Jess and the Manx tabby with Postman Pat at Laxey Wheel; the 36p value with a Viking warrior and his longboat at Peel harbour.

Cats featured again on stamps, produced in 1995 for release in early 1996. These depict Manx cats bought on the Island and then taken abroad by breeders. The 1996 set of stamps are reproduced on the inside front cover.

Colleen Corlett   1994   Cartor

20   ISLE of MAN

© IOMPO / WA

Colleen Corlett   1994   BDT

A Manx - Dutch Family

A Manx cat family in the Netherlands: They belong to the Cattery van Manxdrecht, one of a number of catteries in the Netherlands specialising in Manx and exporting them all over Europe, America and Canada. Active catteries include 'Noah's Ark' run by the family Verlaan and 'Breaside' run by the family van der Veen.

The ginger and white tom pictured here is eight year old Tattleberry Lewys. The pure white is Tattleberry Fflurr, also the same age. Taking a stroll is three year old Ballakayt Meeily. The wide-eyed kitten is eleven week old Carron, daughter of Lewys and Meeily.

According to Jan Kop of Cattery van Manxdrecht "Manx cat people are a bit strange. They don't listen to others too much and go their own way. Let's be honest, when all the other breeders with fine Siamese and Persian cats with the most beautiful colours are showing their best results and you are going to the judge's table with a farmer's cat which is missing one of the most important parts...well, there must be something wrong with you. But proud we are!"

Jan says everyone always asks him at cat shows: "How did you take off the tail?"

When explaining for the 50,000th time, he says, "you sometimes whisper: 'With a rusty knife on a stone!' You should see those faces!"

Manx Beauties

New coloured Manx cats with Persian blood in their ancestry were introduced in the early 1990s by Foxdale breeder Mary Hughes. Yched Nane, pictured here at five months, was believed to be the first Lilac Point Manx in Britain.

The one with a brown face, ears and paws is Apple, a Chocolate Tortie Point Manx, pictured when about 12 months old. She got her name because her head was thought to resemble an apple when she was born.

A Self-Chocolate was born but died.

Pictured lying down at the age of nine months is the yellow-eyed Rhencullen Lass, believed to be the first Self-Lilac Manx in Britain. Mrs Hughes calls her 'Lilo Lill.'

What's usually known as ginger in Britain is red in America. Here's an example - a tabby tom - a seven month old Clacritter Pyndar (pronounced Clay-critter) bred by Leslie Falteisek of Little Canada, Mn who produced a number of National CFA Manx wins in the 1980s.

Tail – Ender

Finally . . . the motto here is very apt for Manx cats. "He Laughs Loudest Who Stays Longest." The cat's entitled to the grin, illustrated here in a 1909 cartoon. Repeatedly written-off as about to become extinct his descendants have made come-backs that have amazed the "experts."

In 1995 there was even a three-car racing team named after them. The "Manx Cats" actually had tails. They were classic touring Jaguars entered in a saloon car racing championship by Manx businessmen Trevor Baines, Alan Lloyd and Grahame Warwick. The team name and grinning cat logo was intended to refer to the Jaguars. They were "big cats from Man" after all. But outside specialised motoring circles there can be no doubt what others thought.

For a racing team to adopt the name indicates that no matter what some critics say, the Manx Cat no longer suffers from an image of being a weak, delicate and pitiable thing.

The cartoon below captures the true spirit: a tough, resilient prankster of the feline world.

In truth there's only one thing wrong with the Manx and that's its name. Strictly speaking it should be Manks. There's no X in the Isle of Man's Gaelic language!

He Laughs Loudest who Stays Longest.

Hi Kelly ! ! is a wondrous cry,
It tells when all else fails :

And refers to the pranks
In the land of the Manx,
Where the cats have got no tails.

Published by
**The Manx Experience,
45 Slieau Dhoo, Tromode Park,
Douglas, Isle of Man, IM2 5LG**
Copyright
Robert Kelly ©
Scanning and printing by
**Mannin Media Group Limited,
Spring Valley Industrial Estate,
Braddan, Isle of Man.**
ISBN 1873120 222